Surfing Virginia Beach
and the Outer Banks

Surfing Virginia Beach and the Outer Banks

TONY LILLIS

THE
History
PRESS

Published by The History Press
Charleston, SC
www.historypress.com

Copyright © 2020 by Tony Lillis
All rights reserved

First published 2020

Front cover, top left: A competitor rounds the marker at the East Coast Surfing Championships in Virginia Beach. *Photo by Buddy Riggs, courtesy of Barbara Eisenberg*; *top right:* The *Virginian-Pilot* wrote of the "blazing wild fashion" of the surfing beach at Virginia Beach. *Photo by Buddy Riggs, courtesy of Barbara Eisenberg.*
Back cover, right: Female surfers wait for their turn to compete. *Photo by Buddy Riggs, courtesy of Barbara Eisenberg.*

Manufactured in the United States

ISBN 9781467145749

Library of Congress Control Number: 2020931991

I would like to dedicate this book to my family—JoAnne, Anna and Emily—and to Mom and Dad and to Grana, all of whom showed tremendous patience and support in the course of putting this book together.

Contents

Acknowledgements

So many people to thank! First among them is Pete Smith, who was instrumental in helping make this book a reality. Thank you, Pete, for your longtime support and for your everlasting stoke! Cowabunga!

Many of my interviews date back more than twenty years, and some who were very helpful in the research of this book are now deceased. To everyone I would like to thank:

Webb Brown, Frank Butler, Bobby Chenman, George Desgain, Peter DeWitt, Michael Dolsey, Bill and Grace Frierson, Hunter Hogan, Bob Holland, Bobby Holland, Bob Irizarry, Lee and Harriet Jones, Wes Laine, Buddy Riggs, Al Roper, Les Shaw, L.G. Shaw, Dawson Taylor, Bill Wells, Paul West, Allen White and Bob White. I also very much want to thank Stewart Ferebee, Shep Jordan, Donna McNelly and Dave Shotton. A special thanks to Barbara Eisenberg, the daughter of Buddy Riggs, for use of her father's photos.

In North Carolina, I am deeply appreciative of Jim Bunch, Scott and Carol Busbey, David "Crockett" Farrow, Larry Gray, Jason Heilig, Jesse Hines, Rascoe Hunt, Keith Newsome, Rick Romano, Murray Ross, Lynn Shell, Bruce Sheppard, Marty Slayton, Jim Vaughn, Jimbo Ward and Steve Wise.

From areas beyond the Mid-Atlantic, a very special thanks to Cecil Lear! I am also sincerely thankful to Dick Catri, Claude Codgen, John Hannon, Mimi Munro, Jack "Murph the Surf" Murphy, Peter Pan, Gary Propper, Kevin Welsh, Dudley Whitman and Bill Yerkes. Thanks to Stuart Parks II and Tama Creef at the Outer Banks History Center; the staff at the Sergeant Memorial Room at Slover Library in Norfolk and at the Virginia Beach Public Library; and William Hazel at the Virginia Beach Surf and Rescue Museum.

I send cheers and fond memories as well to my old surfing buddies Gary Crawford, Greg Haas, Greg Rodriquez, Phil Rodden, Jimmy Vogt, Nick and Chris Lodowski, Michael Chiaramonte, Joe Bozick, Marq Benoit and John Tyrrell. I also want to thank Keith Lown.

And with all my heart I very much want to thank my wife, JoAnne, for her inspiration and incredible support, and my daughters, Anna and Emily. I am also indebted to Dad and Mom and Grana and Uncle John, who always were in my corner no matter what.

Introduction

Virginia Beach and the Outer Banks are quite different from each other, but together they have a few key things in common: the Atlantic Ocean, a surfers' passion for waves and an incredibly rich surfing history.

Virginia Beach is the home to major surfing institutions so iconic and long lasting they are simply referred to as ECSC, WRV and 17th Street. The two surf shops date to the hippie era and also have an immediate presence as one drives onto the Outer Banks. The East Coast Surfing Championships date back even further.

Of course, the Outer Banks has the consistent waves. The barrels. The Lighthouse. The Outer Banks' charms lay not only in its superior swells but also in its relative isolation, its miles of rugged beauty and its history: Blackbeard, shipwrecks, first flight, German U-boats—the 1974 U.S. Surfing Championships.

But far more than that, these two familial regions, ranging from 75 to 150 miles apart—from different states no less—have established themselves both together and individually as major centers of East Coast surfing. (There is Florida to contend with, after all.)

Virginia Beach and the Outer Banks bind together to compose a significant portion of the eastern surfboard manufacturing backbone. Each has produced world-class surfers and shapers, and there has been much cross-pollination between the two areas. To Virginia surfers, you can sometimes double the size of the waves you're riding just by traveling south for two hours. The Outer Banks is easy and close enough for day trips or even to get another surf session in the next morning before heading to work back in Virginia.

They are also tied economically. The supply chain to Hatteras begins in Hampton Roads. The world traveler surfers from the Outer Banks usually come through the Norfolk airport. There are a fair number of homeowners around Hampton Roads who may live mere minutes from the water but actually have their "beach home" somewhere on the Outer Banks, or who eventually moved there permanently. And a decent number from the Outer Banks commute daily to Hampton Roads for their jobs.

Of course, surfers from Virginia Beach have treated the Outer Banks as their own, and for years the Outer Banks and Virginia Beach competed as part of the same ESA district. There have also been contests built around Virginia Beach against Outer Banks surfers. It is possible that over the decades there has been, shall we say, a bit of a rivalry between the two areas.

But both together and separately, as the biggest names in the surfing world passed through this region and as the surfers and shapers from Virginia Beach and the Outer Banks made their marks in the larger surfing world, the two share a heritage that binds them together.

Chapter I

1900-1960

From Duke to Gidget

On the first day of summer in 1912, residents in the small borough of Virginia Beach opened up their *Virginian-Pilot and Norfolk Landmark* newspaper to the headline "Regatta at the Va. Beach Casino…Wave Shooting Contests to Be on Program."

"The fame of the Hawaiian wave shooters has spread around the world and thousands of tourists…have returned home with wonderful tales of the skill the natives show in riding a giant comber to shore on a plank. There is something of the same sort of feat done here every summer day after day that is equally as thrilling to see and far more dangerous and difficult to perform, but there is little heard about it. This is shooting the waves in dories and canoes by young men of the cottage colony at Virginia Beach."

Outrigger canoes had been ridden by the Polynesians for centuries, and all along the East Coast, canoes, dories, ironing boards and mats had been "shooting the waves" since at least the early 1900s. In Virginia Beach, dories had been particularly popular, with team rivalries and annual competitions. Then the lighter canoe made its appearance in the surf and became a hot favorite. The canoe was more challenging and "far more ticklish," and in comparison to the dory, "the danger faced in shooting the waves in the larger craft (Dory) is offset by the skill necessary to negotiate the breaker in a canoe."

Surfboards had also arrived. One of Virginia's earliest surfers was James M. Jordan Jr. His first board was a gift to him from his uncle Walter F. Irvine in 1912 and was "made in Hawaii of redwood, stood about nine feet tall, and weighed 100 pounds," according to *Virginia Beach: A Pictorial History* by

James M. Jordan Jr. of Virginia Beach received this solid surfboard as a gift from his uncle Walter F. Irvine, a wealthy cotton broker, in 1912. Irvine was in the midst of a round-the-world trip and had the board shipped home from Hawaii. Originally it was fourteen to sixteen feet long, but by the time this image was taken in 1918, it had been shortened to make it more manageable to handle. *Courtesy of the Jordan family.*

James Jordan. "The townspeople as well as the guests of the hotels considered Big Jim's surfing ability an exciting feat of skill."

While in Honolulu on an around-the-world tour, Irvine, a wealthy cotton merchant, had a board shipped back to Virginia. It was a very large board, too big it seemed to handle comfortably, so he cut several feet from it.

Back to the contest on that first day of summer, the casino management was planning "a thrilling day's sport at the Beach," a big regatta of rowing races between dory crews, canoe races and sailing races between canoes, as well as "wave shooting contests between both classes of craft."

Two years later, in 1914, the local press noted the advent of "surf boards," as reported in a July 9 headline, "Shooting the Waves on Hawaiian Board Popular."

"The newest sport at the Beach is shooting the waves on a Hawaiian surf board," the story read. "For several seasons canoes have been used for this exciting pastime but one of the Beach colony who recently took a world tour brought back with him a surf board from Honolulu and during the past few days several adventurous swimmers have learned how to master it."

The story also revealed the first surfboard builders were not far behind. "Orders have been placed with local lumber dealers for similar boards," concluding that "this most exciting of water sports seems ready to become a fixture at the Beach."

EARLY SURFING IN NORTH CAROLINA

In North Carolina, surfing may have been introduced even earlier, based on articles published in the mid- to late 1800s along coastal North Carolina and in Charlotte and Raleigh. According to *Surfing NC: A Timeline of the History of the Sport of Surfing in North Carolina* by John Hairr and Ben Wunderly, a number of articles were published in the late nineteenth century about surfing. The Elizabeth City newspaper published an article in 1876 that described surfing and compared a surfboard to a "coffin lid" that was six to nine feet long and two feet wide.

In 1891, the *New Bern Daily Journal* published the surfing adventures of a reporter who called it "one of the most exciting sports imaginable, and I was very quickly initiated into it."

Wrightsville Beach in particular exhibited a growing surf presence. In 1909, the First Annual North Carolina Invitational Tournament was held, featuring "surf board sports, always interesting and entraining for spectators." Then in 1924, a postcard showed someone in the water with a small solid wood surfboard.

According to *Surfing NC*, one of the early surfers in Wrightsville Beach was Burke Bridgers, who saw a *Collier's* magazine article by Alexander Ford Hume about surfing and wrote back asking about surfboard design and plans. Hume himself became rather famous as a promoter of surfing at a time when the sport was waning in popularity in Hawaii. Hume was from South Carolina originally and lived there into his late thirties but moved to Hawaii in the early 1900s.

Though not located on the Outer Banks, Wrightsville Beach, North Carolina, exhibited a growing surf presence, evidenced from a 1924 postcard showing someone in the water with a small solid wooden surfboard. *Author's collection.*

In 1908, he founded the prestigious Outrigger Canoe Club and around that time showed author Jack London how to surf. Subsequently, London wrote an article titled "Surfing: A Royal Sport," which further helped surfing to gain mass consciousness.

Hume likely influenced the development of surfing along the East Coast even before Duke Kahanamoku came over for the first time in 1912. Documentation exists from 1911, for instance, of surfing around Morehead City and Beaufort on the southern Outer Banks.

DUKE SURFS EAST COAST ON WAY TO OLYMPICS

It was in 1912 that Duke Kahanamoku, the great Hawaiian swimmer and surfer, first demonstrated surfing in front of curious and eager easterners. On his way to Stockholm to swim for the United States at the Olympics, he stopped in New York, where he is reported to have bodysurfed at Far Rockaway and Sea Gate. While there, it was reported he generated considerable enthusiasm from his demonstrations, and a kid from New Jersey named Sam Reid took up the burgeoning sport.

Duke trained in Philadelphia, and on his way back from the Olympics, he surfed at Atlantic City and Ocean City, New Jersey. He returned east in 1920 on his way to the Amsterdam Olympics, where he lost to Johnny "Tarzan" Weissmuller. On the way, Weissmuller and Kahanamoku gave a swimming exhibition at Belmar, where presumably, if any waves existed at all, surfing was also performed in front of the beach crowds.

Duke reportedly also traveled to Narragansett, Rhode Island, where he surfed at Scarborough Beach. At the time, Narragansett was a summer resort known not only for its grand hotels but also the famed Narragansett Casino.

Rumors have abounded as passed down through the decades by some credible sources that Duke may have visited Nags Head and perhaps even Virginia Beach. But there is no documentation from newspapers or otherwise to verify it.

More likely, according to *Surfing NC*, Hawaiian entertainer Willie Kaiama gave a surfing demonstration in Nags Head in August 1928 as part of a celebration of Virginia Dare Day. Newspaper accounts indicate that Kaiama and his fellow performers may have also visited Virginia Beach as part of an East Coast tour.

While Duke Kahanamoku is largely given credit for introducing the sport to the East Coast on his 1912 trip, in various forms the sport had already arrived. In beach towns along the Eastern Seaboard, solid mahogany and redwood boards, usually about eight to nine feet and weighing 100 to 125 pounds, could be seen. These boards were either shipped or brought back from trips to California or Hawaii or built locally. Surfing began sinking its meager roots primarily in New York, New Jersey, Virginia, North Carolina and Florida.

In 1924, Duke again traveled to Atlantic City to demonstrate the sport on his way to the Olympics. Meanwhile, all over New Jersey, the kids and tourists rode waves on actual ironing boards that they bought in hardware stores. A craze strengthened along the New Jersey Shore, and ironing boards were the standard for wave riding. The ironing boards were approximately five feet long by about eleven and a half inches wide and made of redwood, and many times they had handle holds on them. People actually stood on them when riding, and they were sometimes used as lifesaving boards as well.

Estimates were that probably a couple hundred boards across the state were being used for surfing. However, ironing boards presented a hazard. When you wiped out on a wave or lost your grip, they washed ashore, hitting bathers. Subsequently, they were outlawed. It wouldn't be the last time.

Mats also were a popular way to ride waves but became hard to get during World War II because rubber was a vital commodity for the war effort. Dories and Lapstrake boats, sixteen feet long, were utilized to ride waves. These were ridden after the war years, along with the ironing boards and surf mats, which came in four- and six-footers.

Through the 1910s and '20s, different forms of wave riding existed in Virginia Beach. "We had these little chest boards," remembered Peter DeWitt, who grew up in Virginia Beach in the 1920s. "Then they had these solid boards, those who were lucky enough to get hold of them."

"John Smith had a solid surfboard, which was pretty small, I guess it was eight feet," remembered Bob Holland. "It was solid, square. And they had some that were laminated and mahogany or redwood and balsa wood… same thing, solid. But they were around, and people got into riding these paddleboards."

TOM BLAKE MEETS DUKE

In the 1920s, surfboard design started to progress due to a man by the name of Tom Blake. Blake was from Wisconsin and by chance met Duke

Kahanamoku in Detroit in 1920, around the time Blake graduated high school. Inspired by Duke, Blake moved to California in 1921 and over time began swimming, lifeguarding and surfing.

According to Tom Blake biographer Gary Lynch, Blake became a long-distance swimming champion for the Los Angeles Athletic Club by winning an AAU ten-mile swim up the Delaware River in Philadelphia. He also won several West Coast swim meets.

In 1924, Blake became an ocean lifeguard for the Santa Monica Swim Club. Duke happened to also be a lifeguard there, and between 1924 and 1927, Duke and Blake worked together and became friends. This is when Blake started learning to surf. Blake's swimming career continued on for several years, and he also served as a stunt double in Hollywood movies, performing in dozens of films over two decades, according to Lynch.

Lynch wrote that Blake traveled to Florida for the first time in 1922 to be a stunt double in a film called *Where the Pavement Ends*. "They made me wrestle with a dead shark in that film," Blake is reported to have said. While there, he reportedly tried riding a short solid redwood board someone had. But this was before he actually knew how to surf.

In 1924, when he was twenty-two, Blake went to Hawaii for the first time, where he learned to surf with the help of some of Kahanamoku's friends. He also spent a lot of time in the Bishop's Museum studying the old Hawaiian surfboards. Blake started making boards modeled on these old Hawaiian boards, which he made out of solid wood or with alternating strips of laminated pine or redwood. All the boards were heavy.

Blake's goal was to make these solid boards lighter. He first did this by drilling dozens of holes in his solid sixteen-foot board, which reportedly trimmed as much as fifty pounds. Then he covered it with a thin layer of wood.

Solid boards, however, were still the standard when two years later, in September 1926, Blake and New Jersey native Sam Reid traveled to Malibu, where Blake was the first to surf the famous point break using a ten-foot solid hardwood board. Reid was the kid who was at Sea Gate, New York, in 1912 when Duke demonstrated surfing; he and Blake had become friends.

Then in August 1928, the first ever Pacific Coast Surf Board Championships were held in Corona Del Mar. At this meet, Blake brought the board in which he had drilled dozens of holes. On this much lighter board, he won the paddling contest going away.

This led him to design and build the first "hollow" board, built with a framework, kind of like a boat, which he then covered with plywood. Blake started developing new ways to create lighter surfboards using new materials like plywood. Not only were these boards lighter, but they also paddled much faster and made it easier to catch waves.

"Blake had developed this hollow board with ridges in it and a center board and the sides were covered with strips of mahogany," remembered Peter DeWitt from Virginia Beach, "and he had gone to Hawaii and was trying to get it promoted, to get someone to back him with it, but he couldn't get anybody."

"It was there he entered the Hawaiian paddleboard race and won the title. They sort of ran him off the island. He ended up in Miami, and that's where he met the Whitman brothers, Bill and Dudley, and the lifeguards from Virginia Beach John Smith, Dusty Hinnant and Babe Braithwaite."

Tom Blake made regular trips to the East Coast, where he traveled from town to town demonstrating his paddleboard. Blake spent his life as a professional lifeguard, and he moved with the seasons, living out of his car, and traveling to the East during summers, picking up work and marketing his paddleboards.

In 1931, Blake filed an application with the U.S. Patent Office for his paddleboard, which was granted on August 16, 1932. The patent noted that the paddleboards were an average of twelve feet long by twenty-three inches wide by three inches thick, flat on top and slightly rounded on the bottom, with rounded edges and weighed about one hundred pounds.

His board was initially manufactured by the Los Angeles Ladder Company and purchased along the East Coast for use by lifeguards, the Red Cross and surfers.

Blake spent considerable time demonstrating surfing techniques and his paddleboard's uses for ocean rescues. In 1938, Wrightsville Beach purchased a "Hawaiian made surfboard for use by the lifeguards," though it is not known if it was Blake who sold the board. Many beaches along the East Coast, particularly along New Jersey and Long Island, adopted the Blake board, and Blake spent his summers lifeguarding in Babylon, Gilgo Beach and Jones Beach.

HISTORY OF VIRGINIA BEACH

In 1607, English explorer John Smith landed at what he called Cape Henry in what is now Virginia Beach, before moving across the Chesapeake Bay and up the James River to establish Jamestown.

ALBEMARLE HALL provides every modern convenience for the comfort of guests. Facing the ocean are spacious verandas where one may sit for hours drinking in the expanse of beauty reaching to the horizon.

For appetites whetted by the salt ocean breezes Albemarle Hall's skilled chefs offer delicious meals, including all varieties of sea food. Special Dining Room for Children under direct supervision of a dietician.

Albemarle Hall is under ownership management. Guests are immediately impressed with the cordial and hospitable atmosphere, and the sincere desire of every member of the staff to make your stay memorably pleasant. A growing clientele numbers many who return year after year to enjoy the genuine hospitality. A vacation at Virginia Beach and at Albemarle Hall offers an ideal outing, where nature is lavish in her gifts and the pleasure of your stay brings health and happiness.

For Reservations, Write, Telegraph or Telephone
ALBEMARLE HALL
(AMERICAN PLAN)
J. STANLEY SMITH, Managing Owner
Ocean Front of 24th Street
Virginia Beach, Virginia
Local and Long Distance Telephone 120
Garage Connections   Parking Facilities

THE MIRAMAR, at South Palm Beach, Florida,

Albemarle Hall at 24th Street was a cottage hotel in Virginia Beach from the 1920s owned by Stanley Smith. In 1929, his son John Smith met Dusty Hinnant at school in North Carolina. Hinnant had lifeguarding experience and spent summers lifeguarding at the Albemarle. In those days, hotels provided the lifeguards, who earned money through beach concessions such as renting chairs, umbrellas and rafts. *Courtesy of Pete Smith.*

One hundred years after John Smith landed, Blackbeard is said to have tucked inside the Chesapeake Bay on his pillaging forays up the Atlantic coast from his home base in Ocracoke and to hang out by Lynnhaven Inlet and the waters behind what is now Chic's Beach.

Decades after that, due to increasing numbers of shipwrecks, the Cape Henry Lighthouse was built in 1792. In 1878, the Seatack Lifesaving Station was built at 24th Street. After the first lighthouse was deemed to have structural problems, a second lighthouse was completed in 1881.

In 1880, some Norfolk and Princess Anne citizens built a clubhouse near what is now 17th Street on the ocean. In 1882, they formed a company and built a twenty-mile track from Norfolk to the ocean. Then in 1883, they opened the Virginia Beach Hotel, which after improvements in 1888 they renamed the Princess Anne Hotel. A boardwalk was built between 12th and 16th Streets the same year in front of the hotel. Development from there moved north and south along "cottage row."

Albemarle Hall at 24th Street was a cottage hotel from the 1920s owned by Stanley Smith, who had a son named John Smith. In those days, hotels

John Smith, Dusty Hinnant, Hugh Kitchin and Buddy Guy were lifeguards in Virginia Beach who helped pioneer surfing and began the lifeguard service and beach concession. *Courtesy of Pete Smith and the Hinnant Family Collection at the Virginia Beach Surf and Rescue Museum.*

See the Lifeguard

For the rental of Beach Umbrellas, Chairs and Surf Riders.

Your friendly Life Guard is for your greater protection

and enjoyment of the Beach and Surf.

North and South

Umbrella Beach Service

The Virginia Beach Lifesaving Service was started in 1930, followed by the Virginia Beach Lifeguard Association in 1932, which was approved by the town council to provide lifeguard services. Later, they broke off into the North and South. *Courtesy of Pete Smith.*

provided the lifeguards, who made their money by renting out beach concessions, including chairs, umbrellas and rafts.

Smith's son, John Smith, and Graham "Dusty" Hinnant were friends at Oak Ridge Military Institute in Raleigh. Hinnant had previous experience lifeguarding at a lake and was Red Cross certified. Smith invited Hinnant to Virginia Beach in 1929 to work at the Albemarle Hall as a lifeguard. Hinnant then began training lifeguards.

As more cottage hotels were built and more people came to the resort, Hinnant and Smith started providing lifeguarding services for the whole beach, along with Buddy Guy and Hugh Kitchin.

Later on, the service split at 25th Street into the North Umbrella Beach Service, run by Hinnant and Hugh Kitchin, and the South Umbrella Beach Service, run by John Smith and Buddy Guy.

SMITH AND HINNANT GO TO FLORIDA

Smith at the time had a solid board, which was the standard then, and there were a few of those around. James Jordan Jr. had the board his uncle had sent him from Hawaii and others had made their own boards. Hunter Hogan had traveled to Hawaii, renting one from Duke himself at the Outrigger Canoe Club, and he kept a board at the North End.

In the winter of 1930, Smith, Hinnant and M.F. "Babe" Braithwaite loaded up the solid mahogany board and took what would be the first of many annual trips to Florida, bypassing Nags Head and the Outer Banks but stopping at points along the East Coast to surf, including the Carolinas, Daytona and Palm Beach, before heading to Miami.

While in Miami Beach, they met Vic Simmons, a lifeguard who worked the Indian Creek Apartments beach concession. Simmons offered tips about his concession business, and before long, according to Pete DeWitt, John Smith owned concessions on thirteen different beach locations from Rehoboth Beach, Delaware, to Galveston, Texas.

Each year after the Virginia Beach summer season, Smith and Hinnant journeyed to Miami to set up and run a cabana service in nearby Delray Beach. Like previous trips, they brought with them a ten-foot Hawaiian solid surfboard. Upon arrival, they drove over the causeway to Miami Beach and the ocean off 41st Street, where they took turns riding it.

Meanwhile, Bill Whitman and Dudley Whitman, two brothers from Miami Beach, had been riding waves on mats and belly boards as kids on

Three lifeguards and two unidentified women pose with three paddleboards. *Left to right*: John Smith, Bill Cox and Dusty Hinnant. *Courtesy of Pete Smith and the Hinnant Family Collection at the Virginia Beach Surf and Rescue Museum.*

Lake Michigan and Miami Beach. According to Dudley, these were beautiful boards that Bill, five years older and quite a craftsman, had made. At the time, they had never ridden an actual surfboard. Seeing what the three Virginians brought down, a real surfboard, amazed the Whitman brothers, who were quite a bit younger than Smith and Hinnant, and Bill and Dudley wasted no time in making friends with the Virginia surfers.

Smith let them try his board on the surf in 1932, which allowed Dudley and Bill to have their first experiences catching waves on a surfboard and riding them to the beach. After a few wipeouts and ungainly loss of balance, they got the hang of it.

With this firsthand experience, Bill Whitman constructed a similar board. Using a plank of lightweight sugar pine, he shaped it in much the same way as an ancient Hawaiian board. When hoisted, the ten-foot board weighed eighty-seven pounds and was painted white, with a red lightning bolt inscribed on the top of its deck. Following completion of Bill's board, a month or so later, younger brother Dudley built a twelve-foot solid redwood surfboard. This slid sideways until he shortened its length by two feet. Then it rode better.

In 1932, while Dudley was busy in the workshop where they built their boards, outside Tom Blake was paddling offshore on one of his famous hollow boards. The Whitmans introduced themselves, and not long after Smith and Hinnant met Blake.

Blake traveled a lot, and he came east every year or two, staying in Miami Beach, sometimes with the Whitmans. He also visited coastal towns up the East Coast, demonstrating the lifesaving qualities of his board as well as his surfing abilities and he also developed buoys and other items to aid in rescuing people.

He continued to shave as much weight as possible, to develop lighter boards made with a frame, rounded edges and a pointed tail. In 1935, Blake came up with an early version of the fin that helped stabilize the board and increased maneuverability. The same year, Blake published a book called *Hawaiian Surfboard* and another titled *Hawaiian Surfriders* and had a surfing photo spread in *National Geographic*. In 1937, he followed that up with the famous article in *Popular Mechanics* titled "Riding the Breakers." Word started getting around the country about surfing and how to build a surfboard, not just in coastal areas but in the mainstream as well.

Bill Whitman learned that Blake's plans to his hollow board were currently appearing in *Popular Mechanics* magazine. Using this as a guide, Bill built his first Blake board. "It was made of mahogany with hollow ribs, twelve feet nine inches long, about twenty-two inches at its widest point. Holding it together were brass screws. These were countersunk into the planking with cold water putty covering over the screw hole."

Right: Prince Butler poses on the beach with a paddleboard. *Courtesy of Frank Butler.*

Below: Even though they were much lighter than solid wood surfboards, paddleboards were still big and heavy. Frank Butler demonstrates the shoulder carry. *Courtesy of Frank Butler.*

Prior to starting construction, Bill brought out a set of full-size plans. "With these drawings to work from, it was an easy task to cut each piece of wood so that it would fit exactly where it was supposed to go. Several coats of tung oil varnish applied after a thorough sanding completed the job."

"The finished board performed unbelievably well," remembered Dudley. "When paddled, each stroke moved it forward about twelve feet, and after attaining speed as it moved effortlessly over the water." Following completion of Bill's board, younger brother Dudley, only thirteen at the time, built his first hollow board.

The two Whitmans experimented with ways to build boards. They innovated the use of marine glues and wooden dowels to join the board together. With wooden dowels, the board could have rounder edges than those that used screws. They also greatly improved its appearance and performance. Because the boards filled with water after while, a plug was added to drain the boards.

SMITH AND BRAITHWAITE INTRODUCE SURFBOARDS TO DAYTONA BEACH

Gaulden Reed was born in 1918, and when he was growing up in Daytona Beach, everybody had a body board, about four feet in length. "We would put together slabs of cypress and they were like current boogie boards." They would also ride "oomiaks" in the surf, which were like kayaks and popular at that time.

In 1932, John Smith and Babe Braithwaite passed through town on their way to Miami Beach and caused quite a stir with their surfboards. They set up a beach concession there, where Reed worked for a couple winters. That year, based on what he'd seen from the Virginia Beach guys, Reed made his own first surfboard of cypress with mahogany on the front and back and plywood on top. He used nails to hold it together. Of course, it leaked, but he continually refined his board.

Year after year, Smith and Hinnant and for a while Braithwaite traveled south to Florida in the offseason. Dusty Hinnant ran a cabana service in Fort Lauderdale for forty years. According to the *South Florida Sun Sentinel*, it was Hinnant who was "one of the first people to introduce the sport of surfing to Florida.…He and a friend came down to Fort Lauderdale and stopped at Daytona Beach to do some surfing. People there had never seen surfboard before," his wife, Lorraine, said.

Back in Virginia Beach, one of the popular rentals at the time was the Hodgeman float, which came in four-foot and six-foot sizes. These were striped and made of heavy fabric. The best swimmers, including Hunter Hogan, Mary Welton and others, went out during northeasters and rode these floats, pumped up with as much air as possible.

But word was getting around about the new Tom Blake paddleboard, which had just been patented. "Around 1932," Peter DeWitt remembered, "I had Mr. Caffey down on 9ᵗʰ Street make a board. He was a carpenter. It was a hollow board, which I gave him the plywood, a blue board that I had for two years and then sold it to Goody Taylor…J. Goodenow Taylor. And then in 1934, when Bill Cox called us together that he had gotten those plans from Tom Blake, via John Smith."

By the winter of 1934–35, when Tom Blake made a trip to Miami, John Smith owned the concessions on thirteen different beaches from Delaware to Texas, and he knew Tom Blake pretty well by then. Smith got a set of the plans directly from Blake to build paddleboards and contacted Bill Cox, with the understanding that he would make two sets of the boards for Hinnant and Smith.

In Bill Cox's basement on 11ᵗʰ Street and Atlantic Avenue, Bill's brother Budd, Pierre Croonenberghs and Peter DeWitt each built one and cut out two extra sets for the boards. Smith and Hinnant constructed those eleven-foot boards later in the restaurant of the Albemarle Hall, which closed in the winter and didn't open up again until spring.

Blake's plans were originally drawn on a sheet of wrapping paper, with little regard to materials and scale. Cox was an engineer and set out to do the plans as an engineer would, with proper specifications and with the goal of getting the bugs out of the design.

Cox went to Langley Air Force Base in Hampton and talked about materials with engineers there. They gave him a guidance on glues, sealants and hydro and aero dynamics. Boards had a tough time staying watertight, and "you spent most of the time drying it out." One of their first innovations was a U-joint to help keep water out. All the boards had a plug so you could empty the water from them after surfing.

In 1937, Hogan took a trip to Miami, where he met up with Smith, Hinnant and Braithwaite. Back in Virginia Beach, Tommy Scott, a lifeguard, advocated the board's benefits as a lifesaving device and built one for seventy-five dollars after going to a camp and seeing its uses. Scott and Hogan stripped down the board and put eight coats of varnish on it, and Hogan surfed it. Then, just prior to World War II, it was stolen.

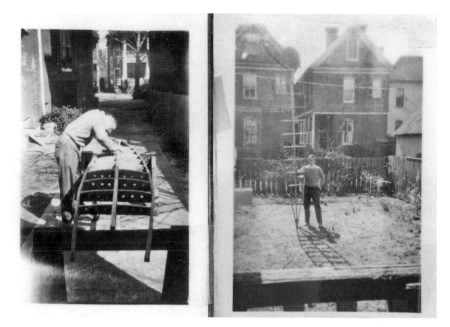

John T. Ferebee lived on Raleigh Avenue in the Ghent section of Norfolk and during summers was a Virginia Beach lifeguard. He is shown here building a paddleboard in his backyard and holding up the completed frame. *Archive of John Terrell Ferebee, www. stewartferebee.com.*

Meanwhile, in Norfolk, John T. Ferebee lived in Ghent on Raleigh Avenue and was a lifeguard during summers on the North End. He built a board based on the Blake article in *Popular Mechanics* and surfed it during the 1940s and 1950s.

Ferebee was introduced to surfing by Mason Gamage, also from Norfolk, who was a few years older and also had built a paddleboard. Tommy Bond, a cousin of Ferebee's who lived near Larchmont, was another who built a board.

In the 1930s on Colley Avenue in Norfolk—in what used to be the Old Dominion Paper Company and after that the Atlantic Ordnance and Gyro Ship Repair (and now the Mill Lofts at ODU)—was what was noted as a "surfboard production manufacturing studio."

Until the end of the 1940s, the Blake-style board replaced the old spruce pine and redwood solid planks, which weighed about 125 pounds. Boards went from 125 to 150 pounds in the 1920s to 75 to 100 pounds in the 1930s based on the new Blake design.

Babe Braithwaite was considered probably the best surfer in Virginia Beach at that time. He was the youngest of three brothers, hence the

John T. Ferebee poses with a board he built in Norfolk. The wording at the top, "Coquette," means "flirt" or "flirtatious" in French, which may have been inspired by the nose-art of World War I–era airplanes. *Archive of John Terrell Ferebee, www.stewartferebee.com.*

name "Babe." At the time, Babe had the beach concession in front of the Marshall's Hotel on 66th Street. He built his boards with a guy named Bob Barco, and all had his name "Babe" at the top. Very athletic, he was known to surf under a full moon at night.

"NOVEL SURFBOARD COMPETITION"

In 1932, according to Blake biographer Lynch, Tom Blake participated in a twenty-six-mile California paddleboard race from Point Vicente to Catalina Island and also paddled the mouth of San Francisco Bay.

One of the first surfing contests to take place in Virginia Beach—and, according to one newspaper, the first on the East Coast—was a surfboard paddling race across the mouth of the Chesapeake Bay. The *Virginia Beach News* reported in a September 13, 1935 article, "Beach Life Guards to Sponsor Novel Surfboard Competition."

Among those in the contest was Babe Braithwaite, who also operated at that time a beach concession in front of the Courtney Terrace hotel. He had a little hut beside the hotel where he rented the paddleboards.

The first surfboard race to be staged on the Atlantic coast, and to our knowledge, the first such competition ever planned for American waters, will be held this coming Sunday morning over a 26-mile course from Cape Henry to Cape Charles. Life guards who have worked at Virginia Beach during the past season will compete.

Scheduled to participate in the race were Braithwaite, R.L. Etheridge, Bill Cox, Tony Burke, Dusty Hinnant and George Clark. The event was expected to take four to five hours. The hope was that this would be the first of many races in which "noted surfboard champions of the world would be invited to participate." This, however, counted as the first and last such event.

A tremendous tide roars between these two points, sweeping out into the open ocean, and no swimmer has ever been known to master the distance. Gertrude Ederle and others who have mastered the English Channel have attempted to negotiate this stretch, but always without success. As the crow flies, the airline distance is fourteen miles, but a direct course is impossible because of the tides.

It would be far more than simply a direct course. "They had quite a strong current pulling them out. It was very dangerous," recalled Peter DeWitt. The next week's edition of the *Virginia Beach News* gave the result with an ominous headline: "Dense Fog Hampers Contestants; Accompanying Boat in Distress."

Completing the difficult passage from Cape Henry to Cape Charles in the record of six hours and fifty one minutes, M.F. "Babe" Braithwaite of Virginia Beach last Sunday won the first surfboard competition ever to be sponsored in the waters of the Atlantic. Estimating the distance traversed as approximately twenty miles, Braithwaite spent most of this seven hours in the midst of a dense fog, guiding his course by the partially hidden rays of the sun and the barking of the cape's foghorn.

Only two others competed in the race—Robert L. Etheridge and George Clark, both of Virginia Beach—with the rest of the contestants

Virginia ...

A Journal Devoted to the Interests

VIRGINIA BE...

Braithwaite Leads Surfboard Competition To Cape Charles

Bids for Farm Loans Show Big Increase

The Farm Credit Administration said yesterday production credit loans are running double what they did last year.

It said 560 production credit associations in the first eight months this year loaned $177,-000,000 compared with $56,-000,000 in the corresponding 1934 period.

The amounts for the eight-month periods by districts included, (the first figure is 1934 and the second 1935):

Baltimore, Md.; Pennsylvania, Maryland, Delaware, Virginia, West Virginia, $3,209,-000 and $4,181,000.

4-H CLUBS PLAN FALL ACTIVITIES

Council Acts to Sponsor Poultry Tattooing Among the Farmers of County.

Dense Fog Hampers Contestants; Accompanying Boat In Distress.

Completing the difficult passage from Cape Henry to Cape Charles in the record time of six hours and fifty-one minutes, M. F. Braithwaite, of Virginia Beach, last Sunday won the first surfboard competition ever to be sponsored in the waters of the Atlantic. Estimating the distance traversed as approximately twenty miles—the airline distance between both lights is fourteen miles—Braithwaite spent most of his seven hours in the midst of a dense fog, guiding his course by the partially hidden rays of the sun and the barking of the-cape's foghorn.

Two Others Compete

Robert Etheridge and George Clark, Jr., both of Virginia Beach, where they were employed as life guards during the summer, also undertook the strenuous competition. Losing their course because of the fog, they landed about three miles south of the town of Cape Charles, completing their abbreviated "swim" some distance

Left: A story in the *Virginia Beach News* covered the paddleboard race across the mouth of the Chesapeake Bay. It reported that Babe Braithwaite was not only the winner but also the only one to finish. *Author's collection.*

Below: Many considered Babe Braithwaite, winner of the 1935 paddling contest across the mouth of the Chesapeake Bay, to be one of the best surfers in Virginia Beach at that time. *Courtesy of Frank Butler.*

withdrawing because of the weather. "Losing their course because of the fog, they landed about three miles south of the town of Cape Charles, completing their abbreviated 'swim' some distance short of the agreed goal," reported the paper.

> *Braithwaite, who was awarded a cup by the Cavalier Hotel for his accomplishment, launched his board together with the other two contestants, about 7 o'clock in the morning. The fog was heavy and, although the tide was high at the time of the launching, the ebb was apparent before the boards had traversed one mile of water. Braithwaite pulled away from his companions, choosing a northerly route, from which he bore down on the goal. His accomplishment makes him the first man ever to reach Cape Charles from Cape Henry under his own power.*

SURFERS GO TO WAR

Born in 1928, Bob Holland grew up in Virginia Beach on 24th Street. His dad, Robert Barrett Holland, had a couple of boards that were, of course, big and heavy. When he was about nine or ten years old, Bob used to drag one to the beach and started learning to surf before World War II.

"It was about 10 feet long, no fin, mahogany with spruce sides and weighed 100 pounds or so. I'd put it on a wagon and drag it to the water," he told *Eastern Surf* magazine.

Meanwhile, Dusty Hinnant continued to be an innovator in beach concessions. In 1940, when air mattresses were first coming on the scene, he worked with Converse in New York to design the Dusty Hinnant Rent-a-Float and began renting them at beach concessions from Virginia to Florida.

Hinnant was also featured in an advertisement for Noxzema skin care cream as the expert lifeguard from Virginia Beach. "Beach tested by lifeguards at many famous Beaches!" claimed the ad. "G. Dusty Hinnant, Captain, Virginia Beach, Va. says 'We've used Noxzema here for years. It brings fast relief and helps heal even the most severe cases of sunburn.'"

After the war, the number of surfers in Virginia Beach grew. "I guess it was fifty or less," said Dawson Taylor. Hunter Hogan, Bill Cox, Bill Drinkwater and Jack Meredith were some of the surfers then, along with the next generation of Bob Holland, Clay Perry, Dave Scarmont, Jimmy Hatcher, Clint Walker and Frank Butler. Hogan had surfed in Hawaii and

John Pugh poses on the beach.
Courtesy of Frank Butler.

other areas in his business travels, and he and Charley Lawrence kept a board up at the north end of the beach.

Bob Holland remembered that back in the 1930s, John Smith and Babe Braithwaite would take him out on their paddleboards and put him on their shoulders. As a teenager during World War II, Holland continued to surf at 24th Street, mostly by himself, though there were a handful of others. He also helped out with the beach concessions, gathering up the chairs, umbrellas and floats, and he liked riding the waves on those floats, pumped up as hard as possible.

In the late 1940s, after graduating from Granby High School in Norfolk, Holland followed in his father's footsteps by becoming a Virginia Harbor pilot, responsible for boarding and guiding large ships into the Chesapeake Bay to their docks.

THE OUTER BANKS OF NORTH CAROLINA

Before surfing even got to the Outer Banks, there was already an incredible history there. Ships were sailing past the coast of North Carolina in the early 1500s, long before John Smith settled Jamestown.

In 1585, explorers created a settlement and named it Roanoke Island. A couple years later, John White came over with three ships bringing women and children and then returned to England for supplies. When he finally returned in 1590, everything and everybody was gone. The settlement came to be known as the "Lost Colony."

Over one hundred years later, Blackbeard made Ocracoke his hideout, as he roamed the Gulf Stream from Charleston to Chesapeake Bay pirating ships of their cargo. When Virginia's governor put a bounty on Blackbeard, he was beheaded off Ocracoke Island.

In 1846, two new inlets were opened, one at Hatteras Inlet and another at Oregon Inlet. Then in 1870, the current Cape Hatteras Lighthouse at Buxton was opened, rising 150 feet with its world-famous swirl. Other lighthouses built afterward included those at Bodie Island in 1872 and Currituck Beach in 1875.

Shipwrecks and rescues are a storied part of the Outer Banks, which is known as the "Graveyard of the Atlantic." The dangerous Diamond Shoals is where ships could be drawn in by currents and run aground and then get beat and broken up by northeasters and hurricanes. It is estimated that anywhere from six hundred to one thousand shipwrecks are sunk offshore, including the Civil War battleship the *Monitor*. Following the Civil War, the federal government built twenty-five lifesaving stations along the Outer Banks.

But the Outer Banks has more than just a nautical history. In 1900, Orville and Wilbur Wright made their first trip to Kitty Hawk to test their flying machines. On December 17, 1903, Orville flew for about twelve seconds, and about one hundred feet, in the first flight. In 1931, this historic feat was honored with the construction of the Wright Brothers Memorial. Appropriately enough, an airstrip was built next to it.

Aerial view of the Cape Hatteras Lighthouse in Buxton, North Carolina, circa 1955. *Aycock Brown Collection, courtesy of the Outer Banks History Center.*

View of the new airstrip adjacent to the Wright Brothers Memorial. Notice how sparse the landscape is to the ocean. *Courtesy of the Outer Banks History Center.*

But there is more. During the First World War and World War II, German U-boats prowled off North Carolina, Virginia Beach and the whole East Coast. Blackouts were enforced from Maine to Florida, so as not to identify landmarks to enemy submarines. Enemy subs stalked passing merchant ships, so much so that the waters off Cape Hatteras became known as Torpedo Junction.

EARLY SURFING IN NAGS HEAD

Around 1830, people started coming to Nags Head in the summers, but activity was mostly based on the Albemarle Sound side of the island, where the ferry docked from Elizabeth City and where a hotel was built.

The first oceanside home is reported to have been built in 1855 by a doctor from Elizabeth City. Over the next thirty years, more beach houses were built closer to the ocean, later to be called the Unpainted Aristocracy.

Over the next several decades, homes along the oceanfront continued to be built, owned by nearby farmers and doctors and merchants from Elizabeth City and rural areas in North Carolina and Virginia. This area is now known as the Cottage Row Historic District. At the same time, Nags Head and Cape Hatteras gained a great reputation for fishing, and fishermen came from the Northeast and Florida and around the country.

In 1939, Jennette's Pier in Nags Head was built, the first fishing pier on the Outer Banks. Later, more piers were built, including the Nags Head Pier in 1947, the Kitty Hawk Pier in 1953 and the Avalon Pier in 1958. Piers were later constructed in Rodanthe (1960), Frisco (1962) and Avon (1963). The Bonner Bridge connecting Nags Head to Cape Hatteras National Seashore opened in 1963.

David Stick and his wife, Phyllis, owned the Kitty Hawk Craft Shop, which sold "Juniper Surfboards," according to a 1951 advertisement from the *Coastland Times*. Juniper boards were body boards about three feet long and eighteen inches wide.

In late 1940s, Sherald K. "Gov" Ward from Whaleyville in Suffolk, Virginia, spent summers in Nags Head with his family, body surfing, riding bodyboards and doing a lot of waterskiing. Ward had earned the nickname "Governor" or "Gov" from a mock state election in high school.

After graduating high school in 1948, Ward attended the University of Richmond, where he played football. In the early 1950s, he spent time in the navy, including a year in California. It was in Santa Cruz in 1954 that Gov first discovered surfing.

Born in 1944, Bruce Sheppard grew up across from the Nags Head Pier, part of a family that lived year-round in Nags Head. He was just starting high school in 1958 when Hurricane Helene hovered offshore, kicking up a large swell. Sheppard remembers that Californians Mickey Munoz and Mike Doyle came to town with half a dozen surfboards, and he watched them surfing a huge groundswell "twice out beyond the Nags Head Pier, with them crossing each other and kicking out." He remembers it as the first time he'd seen surfing, and when he asked, they left a board that he kept at his house. Later on, Sheppard bought his first board from Pete Smith at Smith and Holland Surf Shop in Virginia Beach, a ten-foot, two-inch Hanson.

Above: Classic surf woody with surfboard strapped to the top, circa 1938. *Stick family photograph, courtesy of Outer Banks History Center.*

Left: In the 1930s, Captain Tom Fearing of Manteo built a paddleboard that he mainly used for paddling and what was termed "goggle fishing." Here, Fearing and David Stick shared the board, circa 1938. *Stick family photograph, courtesy of the Outer Banks History Center.*

Captain Tom Fearing of Manteo and David Stick out in the surf. *Stick family photograph, courtesy of the Outer Banks History Center.*

View of Buxton looking south from the Cape Hatteras Lighthouse, 1954. *Aycock Brown Collection, courtesy of the Outer Banks History Center.*

THE 1950s

In the 1950s, Californians Hap Jacobs from Redondo Beach, Dewey Weber from Hermosa Beach and Hobie Alter from Laguna Beach, among others, were key influences.

Hobie began selling balsa boards from his family's garage in 1950 and then later from his Dana Point manufacturing operation. By 1958, Hobie and Gordon "Grubby" Clark were making foam and fiberglass surfboards using a new technology called polyurethane. The foam was lighter than the balsa and redwood and was poured into molds to form "blanks," from which boards would be shaped and then fiberglassed. Polyurethane foam blanks revolutionized surfboard quality and design, and Hobie became the leading manufacturer of surfboards.

Hobie also started selling the blanks to other surfboard shapers. He later broke off the foam business and bequeathed that operation to Gordon

Clark, a chemist, who named it Clark Foam. Hobie would make standard and custom boards for famous surfers to promote the Hobie brand, which would soon include Hobie Catamaran sailboats.

Hobie and Dewey Weber, who started producing boards in 1960, along with many others along the way, mass produced boards as quickly as they could to meet a booming California surf market and a burgeoning one on the East Coast. Weber came up with his own innovations, including his famous "hatchet fin."

Meanwhile, surfing began to reach mass appeal through rock-and-roll, including surf guitar star Dick Dale, Jan and Dean and the Beach Boys. Hollywood also captured the beach lifestyle in the form of *Gidget*, a book written in 1957 by a Hollywood screenwriter about his daughter's beach escapades in Malibu. In 1959, the first Gidget movie came out, followed in 1963 by a number of popular "beach party" comedies with such characters as Eric Von Zipper, Bonehead and Big Drop. Of course, there was also Frankie (Frankie Avalon) and Dee Dee (Annette Funicello).

Another type of surf movie was popular also, but mainly just with surfers. A dedicated group of "true" surf moviemakers, including Bud Browne, John Severson and Bruce Brown, made movies more to surfers' liking—hours and hours of footage of incredible surfing in exotic places around the world, with a music soundtrack and maybe a narrator. The most famous of these was *The Endless Summer*.

VIRGINIA BEACH IN THE LATE 1950s

Against this backdrop, in Virginia Beach the seeds for surfing's massive popularity in the next decade were planted by a small group of locals that included Dawson Taylor, Buddy Riggs, Bob Holland and Pete Smith. A West Coast guy named Les Arndt also was important in getting Jacobs surfboards to Virginia Beach.

And much of the old guard was still there as well, including Captain Holland, Hugh Kitchin, Babe Braithwaite and others. John Smith and Buddy Guy opened the Golf Ranch Motel in 1952 on Laskin Road, where Pete Smith would later work the night shift for his uncle John Smith. During the school year, from 1953 to 1958, Pete Smith went to boarding school at Christchurch School and then lived at Albemarle Hall on 24th Street in the summers, helping with the beach concessions as a "float boy," and later becoming a lifeguard himself.

Spurred on by lifeguards who used the paddleboards for lifesaving devices, the sport of surfing became popular in seaside resorts. Here, lifeguards, including Dusty Hinnant, John Smith and Babe Braithwaite, pose with their boards in Virginia Beach. *Courtesy of Pete Smith and the Hinnant Family Collection at the Virginia Beach Surf and Rescue Museum.*

Dusty Hinnant and his wife, Lorraine, lived in Virginia Beach during the summer season but would go to Florida every winter for the next forty years. They first lived in Bahia Mar in Fort Lauderdale on a boat.

In the mid-'50s, Dawson Taylor made a trip to Hawaii after graduating from college. Subsequently, he imported the first balsa wood boards by Velzy/Jacobs and Hanson Surfboards to Virginia Beach. He ordered three or four at a time, collected the money from the buyers and had them shipped together, which saved on costs. In all, he imported no more than a dozen boards, selling them to Hunter Hogan, Bob Holland and others.

In 1957, the *Gidget* movie came out, the story of a girl who hung out on the beach in Malibu and learned to surf. Frank Butler and his brother Prince, along with Forbes Braithwaite and Bob Holland, watched it at the drive-in theater on Laskin Road and were amazed at the "Malibu boards" in the movie and how small and light they were. There was also a fin on the boards that they had not seen before.

Soon after, Les Arndt, a Californian who was stationed at Fort Story, helped surfing expand in Virginia Beach. Arndt knew Hap Jacobs, one of the early California builders. It was through Arndt that Bob Holland

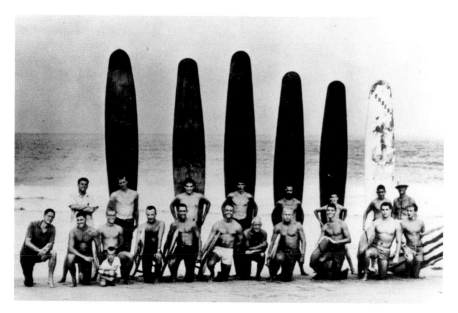

Most if not all the surfers in Virginia Beach at that time gathered for this photograph, circa late 1950s. *Front row, left to right*: Scott Taylor, Bob Holland, Bill Rapp, Johnny Holland (in front of Rapp), Frank Butler, Tommy Bryant, Butch Kitchin, Captain Holland, Waller Taylor, Pete Smith, Bob Gormly and Richard Neal. *Back row, standing, left to right*: Les Arndt, John "Snooker" Turner, Bobby Wainwright, John Pugh, Skip Rawls, Will Pugh, Ricky House and Fred Johnson. *Courtesy of Pete Smith and the Hinnant Family Collection at the Virginia Beach Surf and Rescue Museum.*

brought in some nine-foot, six-inch foam boards, which Holland sold from his garage to Pete Smith and others.

By the late 1950s, mainly from the core group of fifty or so surfers made up largely of lifeguards in Virginia Beach, there were all kinds of surfboards out in the water—from the old wooden ones from the 1930s to the newer balsa boards and the revolutionary polyurethane boards that allowed surfing to boom in the 1960s. Soon, Hobie Alter, Dewey Weber, Bruce Brown, Phil Edwards, Corky Carroll and many others would make their way to Virginia Beach—and that's when surfing really took off.

Chapter 2

The Early 1960s

Surf's Up

In 1960, a man named John Severson made a move called *Surf Fever* and started a magazine called *The Surfer*. In 1961, Phil Edwards named the famed Banzai Pipeline and was the first to surf it. In 1962, the Beach Boys released their first album, *Surfin' Safari*.

Throughout the early '60s, Mickey "Quasimoto" Munoz and Mickey "da Cat" Dora were creating the classic surf style at Malibu, while "beach bikini movies" like *Beach Blanket Bingo* were celebrating a carefree view of beach and surfing life to the rest of America.

Along the Eastern Seaboard, interest was catching. With the benefit of year-round surfing, Florida was the home of a red-hot batch of surfers, with Dick Catri and Jack Murphy in the forefront. In New York, Reuben Snodgrass opened a surf shop and John Hannon started building surfboards. In New Jersey, Cecil Lear organized surfers and fought for beach access. Everywhere, surfing contests were becoming popular.

In Virginia Beach, there existed a fertile culture that helped the sport take off, molded by the steady hand of Bob Holland and the stoke of Pete Smith. On the Outer Banks, Bruce Sheppard, Larry and Ronnie Gray, Jim Bunch, Mike Hayman and Gov Ward pioneered the early surfing scene.

All along the East Coast, there was an emerging group of surfers and an eager batch of shapers who were stoked by *The Endless Summer* and visits by the West Coast surfing elite, the start and evolution of the East Coast Surfing Championships (ECSC) and the exploration and discovery of eastern surf spots, especially on the Outer Banks of North Carolina.

In 1966, it was all chronicled in a cover story in *Sports Illustrated* featuring Phil Edwards surfing the Steel Pier in Virginia Beach that heralded a tremendous eastern phenomenon.

VIRGINIA BEACH: SURFBOARDS AND HARDWARE

In Virginia Beach, surfing was on the verge of taking off. The dawn of the 1960s found Bob Holland selling Jacobs boards from his garage and, soon after, a storefront surf shop. Peter DeWitt and Bill Cox helped build twenty new foam surfboards for a group of boys associated with the Knights Club. Dawson Taylor at Fuel Feed (now Taylor's Do It Center) started selling Hobies, and Buddy Riggs at Western Auto began selling Webers. Bob White, Al Roper and others began shaping boards in their backyards.

Since the late '50s, Bob Holland had sold maybe thirty Hap Jacobs surfboards out of his garage on the North End. In 1961 and 1962, interest in surfing grew with the advent of the new foam boards, and Holland continued to sell Jacobs boards from his garage. Then in the summer of 1962, Holland opened up a storefront during the summer on 18th Street and called it Bob Holland Surf Shop.

Around 1960, a small group of kids spent time during the summer and after school at a place called the Knights Club on 19th Street in Virginia Beach. On weekends, high school kids from all over the area came down for sock hops. During the week, it was a haven and a refuge for boys to get together, box and knock around. Peter DeWitt—who, along with Bill Cox, had built some of those first Blake boards during the 1930s—spent time there helping to build twenty surfboards with the boys.

Meanwhile, Dawson Taylor owned Fuel Feed and Building Supplies on 19th and Arctic. In 1961, he wrote to Hobie Alter about selling his boards in Virginia Beach. "We got our first boards in and built an eight-board rack up in the window." Kids started streaming in, and soon thereafter, Fuel Feed became not only one of the first East Coast Hobie outlets but also one of the biggest distributors of Hobie boards. For $100, you could even get a custom board.

The business built with the local kids, including George Desgain, Bobby Chenman, the McQuilkin brothers and Jimmy Jordan, buying boards. Then, when Hobie ran a full-page ad in *Surfer* magazine showing Fuel Feed as a dealer, Taylor got requests from kids all across the country wanting logos, T-shirts—anything he had.

Buddy Riggs owned the Western Auto hardware store on 17th Street and sold Dewey Weber Surfboards. Here he poses with members of the Weber surf team. Dewey is pictured fourth from left. Riggs also was a prolific photographer who later was elected to the Virginia Beach City Council. *Courtesy of Barbara Eisenberg.*

Two blocks over on 17th Street, Buddy Riggs owned a Western Auto store where he was selling eleven-foot, six-inch and twelve-foot South Pacific surfboards imported from Australia. Riggs had an amusing gimmick to sell them. He put a croquet mallet next to the board and told the kids to take a good swift swing at the thing to see if they could damage the board. But durability didn't replace "shape," and Riggs brought in a variety of boards. One was called the Tiki, a popout board from New York. Popout boards were easily made production models, but they had the hydrodynamics of a telephone pole. Riggs then started getting the surfing magazines and carrying boards by Dewey Weber, Gordon & Smith and Greg Noll. He advertised as the "World's Largest Dewey Weber Surfboard Dealer," and he also carried a "Complete Line of Hang Ten Sportswear." Riggs was also a prolific photographer of the local surf scene.

Farther south of the resort strip, the Enzi family owned a beach cottage in Sandbridge. According to *From the Beach to the Bay: An Illustrated History of Sandbridge in Virginia*, Captain Enzi was stationed in California and brought back a surfboard. It may have been one of the first in the area, where surfing also took off in 1962 and 1963.

HOBIE ALTER WALKS IN

Like many, Pete Smith grew up riding the surf on blow-up mats in the late 1940s and early 1950s. Later, he worked as a helper—a "float boy"—on the beach for his uncle John Smith, a former lifeguard and 1930s pioneer East Coast surfer. During the '50s, after becoming a lifeguard with the Virginia Beach Patrol, Pete also rode some of the big paddleboards. Then, around 1960, he was one of the first in Virginia Beach to get a Jacobs board from Bob Holland.

One night in the fall of 1962, Smith was working at his uncle John's Golf Ranch Motel on Laskin Road when a surprise visitor showed up. Earlier that year, Smith had written an article for *Surfer* magazine called "'Cane Curls," detailing the fantastic hurricane surf in Virginia and North Carolina. He had submitted it on the hotel's letterhead. Alter saw the article and contacted John Severson to find out how to get ahold of Smith. It turns out Hobie was looking for exclusive dealers of his boards.

Hobie Alter and his assistant, Boscoe Burns, showed up one evening when Pete Smith was the night shift manager. Pete was stoked! The next day, they met at Bob Holland's house to come up with a plan, and in March 1963, Smith and Holland Surf Shop opened on 22nd Street as the exclusive Hobie dealer, also carrying Kanvas by Katin and Birdwell Beach Britches.

Pete spent the next few winters working at the Hobie shop in Dana Point doing ding repair and observing the business. He also spent time in Hawaii. Over the years, the shop sponsored surf teams with guys like Bill Frierson, Jimbo Brothers, Edward McQuilkin, Fred Grosskreutz, Norman Grosskreutz and Ronnie Mellott. The big thing for any kid was to get a T-shirt or jacket that said "Hobie Team."

Meanwhile, Bob White first surfed around 1961, when a neighbor bought a surfboard out of the Sears catalogue. Soon after, White set out with a friend to build two boards in his garage. They found a place locally that sold tubular blocks of general foam, and they shaped the board—and then watched the epoxy resin dissolve the foam into the floor. After some trial and error, they had their first boards.

Soon after, White had six Walker blanks shipped in from California, from which he built boards and sold them to neighborhood friends. That gave him enough money to buy his first Skil planer. Then he met up with Al Roper, another board builder, and for a time they had Roper/White Surfboards.

In 1964, Al Roper and Tom Simmons formed Rosi Surfboards out of Roper's garage and made about a half dozen boards, hashing a way to

After Hobie Alter visited Virginia Beach in 1963, Pete Smith (*right*) and Bob Holland (*left*) opened Smith and Holland Surf Shop and became the exclusive Hobie dealer. *Courtesy of Pete Smith.*

The Hobie Surf Team poses at Smith and Holland Surf Shop. *Left to right*: Bill Frierson, Gary Rice and Pete Smith. On the right is Johnny Holland, with Jimbo Brothers in front. *Courtesy of Pete Smith.*

Every surfer aspired to have the Hobie Surf Team logo on his jacket. *Courtesy of Pete Smith.*

start a surfboard shop. In the meantime, the skateboard boom hit. Then in 1965, they opened up Rosi Custom Surfboards at 208 23rd Street, advertising "Quality Custom Surfboards Made in Virginia Beach to Your Specifications." They also sold Wardy boards out of Laguna Beach.

Meanwhile, Simmons had other interests, and Roper bought him out, keeping the name Rosi. The next summer, Roper took on a new partner, Bob White. They became Roper/White Surfboards for a short period. Soon after that partnership was formed, Roper got a draft notice. He was actually ineligible for the draft but, because of a mix-up, had to report to Richmond. Roper got it straightened out, returned to Norfolk and ultimately sold his interest in the shop to White in 1965. Roper soon after moved to California and started working for Hobie Alter. In 1966, Bob White established Bob White Surfboards, with a shop on 23rd Street.

Surfing continued to grow at a phenomenal rate. The surfboard business was booming, and thousands of spectators went to surf contests. According to the *Virginian Pilot* in a 1966 article:

> In 1961, one Beach resident estimated last week, there were all of 11 boards on the beach. In 1962, there were maybe 40–50. In 1963, there were 150 to 200, and in 1964, there were at least 500. Last year there were well over 1000 boards, and the general best estimate this year is that there will be nearly 2000 in the surf or trying to get there. Two thousand boards represents a capital investment in excess of $250,000. Surfing has grown so fast that 20 year olds can talk about the good old days.

THE OUTER BANKS IN THE '60s

Outside Cape Hatteras National Seashore, there were two basic pockets of surfing on the Outer Banks. At the Kitty Hawk Pier were Jim Bunch, Mike Hayman, Earl Jackson and Frank Weeks. At the Nags Head Pier were Bruce Sheppard, Larry and Ronnie Gray and Buster Nunemaker.

Jim Bunch grew up in the 1940s and 1950s in Elizabeth City and spent summers in Kitty Hawk. His main interest was oceanography and diving, so in 1961, he headed off to college at the University of Miami. There he bought his first surfboard, a Hap Jacobs, from West Coast East Surf Shop, and he learned to surf in the orbit of Jack "Murph the Surf" Murphy and Allen Kuhn, the duo who would later go on to steal the Star of India sapphire in New York. During that time, Murphy had his own shop called Murph's Surf Shop.

Bunch brought his Jacobs board back from Miami in 1962 and could be seen surfing at the Kitty Hawk Pier. Mike Hayman, whose family owned the Seafare Restaurant, also had a board, and on any given day Bruce Sheppard,

The March 1962 Ash Wednesday storm battered and flooded Nags Head and Outer Banks. Notice how big the swell looks even from the air. *Aycock Brown Collection, courtesy of the Outer Banks History Center.*

Sherald "Gov" Ward is seen here presenting an Outer Banks Surf Club license plate to Larry Capune from New York, who was attempting to paddle down the East Coast from New York. Standing above Ward is Johnny Midgett. To the left is Mike Hayman. Standing next to Midgett to the right is Jim Bunch. *Aycock Brown Collection, courtesy of the Outer Banks History Center.*

Frank Weeks, Earl Jackson and Johnny Midgett could be seen out surfing. Many worked at the Seafare during the summers.

By the next summer, 1963, surfing had gained popularity in Kitty Hawk, and on the weekends, Bob Holland and members of the Hobie surf team and others were coming down from Virginia Beach.

Farther down the beach in Nags Head, Larry, Tony and Ronnie Gray were the sons of Walter and Stelle Gray of Elizabeth City. Their family owned Gray's department store, and in the summers they lived above the store across from the ocean. As a young guy, Larry Gray had seen Bruce Sheppard and Bob Holland (by now in his mid-thirties) surfing at Nags Head Pier, which was about ten miles from the Kitty Hawk Pier—a long ways away if you didn't yet have a driver's license.

In 1965, Larry Gray was pictured on a postcard riding a nine-foot, six-inch Jacobs that he ordered over the phone from the Jacobs surf shop in California around 1963. Also pictured was his friend Carlton Priest "Buster" Nunemaker, who rode a Greg Noll board.

Some of the oldest families in the area were from Roanoke Island, made up primarily of two towns, Manteo and Wanchese. The locals there were boat builders and fishermen, lifesavers and lighthouse keepers, with old and historic family names like Brown, Farrow, Tillett, Fearing, Daniels and Midgett. Descendants and offspring of these prominent families included Charlie Brown, Robert Midgett, Thomas Daniels, Charlie Fearing, St. Claire Tillett and David Farrow.

Everyone seemed to have a nickname, and David Farrow's was "Crockett." He was from Manteo with deep roots on the Outer Banks. His ancestors were keepers of the Buxton and Bodie Island lighthouses. He started surfing at age eleven in 1965. In the early years, he surfed at Jennette's Pier in Nags Head and Anderson's store in Kitty Hawk, and he got rides to the beach from some of the older surfers, including future state senator Marc Basnight, himself a surfer.

In Buxton, J.C. Conner opened up a little surf shop out of a trailer, and he and Buddy Hooper built some boards. According to *Surfing NC*, Hooper got his first board from his uncle Bill Dillon. In 1966, on the way back to Florida from ECSC, Dick Catri met Hooper, and Catri offered tips on surfboard building. Like many on the Outer Banks, Hooper and Catri were avid fishermen. They enjoyed offshore fishing together. Other surfers included John Ochs and Doug Meekins.

Calvin Burrus, another descendant of Cape Hatteras lighthouse keepers, owned the Texaco station in Buxton, where he sold some Dick

Catri surfboards. His sons Dal, Danny and Don all surfed. Ray Gray, a teacher and principal, surfed, and he introduced his son Landry Gray to the waves. John and Stewart Couch were also avid surfers, and Stewart Couch would travel the world in search of waves. Gary, Don and Andy Bowers were some of the other local surfers. Farther north, in Rodanthe and Salvo, Ervin, Asa Gray and Larry Midgette had the surf to themselves back in the early days.

Gov Ward, after living in California, had started surfing in Kill Devil Hills in the late 1950s. He had Greg Noll and Dewey Weber boards shipped back from California and rode to Norfolk to pick them up. Gov also owned a hotel called the Governor's Inn, which he advertised as "The Gov's In," and he sold and rented some boards there, along with T-shirts and decals. By 1966, he had started making his own boards, called Gov's Surfboards.

Anderson's Beach Store and Grocery was just south of the Kitty Hawk Pier. A sandbar formed in 1964 in front of Anderson's, and surfing moved from the pier to the new beach break. Gov had a deal with Bill Anderson

Surfboards were pretty big back in the day. Vernon Barington and Ralph Wayne "Snooby" Johnson carry a board. *Aycock Brown Collection, courtesy of the Outer Banks History Center.*

Kill Devil Hills from the air, 1965. *Aycock Brown Collection, courtesy of the Outer Banks History Center.*

that he could rent boards in front of his store. It got to be so crowded that out in the waves, Gov Ward started the Gov's Surf Club, otherwise known as the North Carolina Outer Banks Surf Club. Membership provided a license plate attached to your car to park for easy access to the surf. But "Miss Kitty" across the street would let the Wanchese and Manteo surfers park for free in her yard.

Don Bennett also had a little shop by Anderson's. Born in New Bern, Bennett got his first board in 1963 and almost immediately started building Surfboards by Don in a garage in Kitty Hawk near Anderson's, where he also sold and rented out boards. Around 1968, he moved to Virginia Beach for a time, adding to the mix with other board builders like Eastside and West Wind. He opened a Virginia Beach location but soon moved back to Carolina and set up across from the Nags Head Pier.

At the time, Johnny Midgett and George McLain all surfed and hung around Gov's shop, as did Jimbo Ward, who lived in Avalon. Jerry Davis and Les Smith were Kitty Hawk surfers. Davis's father owned Winks, and

A surfer tumbles down a wave, all senses engaged, as he seeks to hang on in the churning surf. *Courtesy of the Outer Banks History Center.*

Smith's dad owned Virginia Dare Hardware. Surfers from the Northeast also came down for early spring warm water and amazingly consistent surf.

There were a number of good female surfers in the '60s, including Bobbie Kennedy from Elizabeth City, Bobby Gill and Marcella Morrisette. Santa Tillett from Manteo was another. And of course, Honey Holland, who spent summers on the Outer Banks was still another.

PHIL EDWARDS AND DEWEY WEBER VISIT THE OUTER BANKS

When Dewey Weber was on the East Coast after the ECSC, he and a group of Californians came down in September 1966 during one of the finest swells. Weber put on a show at the Kitty Hawk Pier in clean curling sizeable surf that impressed the Californians as some of the best they'd seen on the East Coast. Don Carter and Ron Stoner from *Surfer* magazine followed the swell all the way to the lighthouse and ran a story the next year that further cemented the Outer Banks as the home of the East Coast's finest surf.

In 1962 in Nags Head, a laundromat called the Cavalier started renting and selling boards, as well as wax and other items. They kept it a laundromat for many years until much later it became Cavalier Surf Shop. It was almost completely destroyed during the Ash Wednesday storm but resurrected in time for summer beach season.

Floridians Jack Murphy and Dick Catri started coming by on their trips north, staying with Gov Ward at the Governor's Inn. At different times, they both came north for the East Coast Surfing Championships, and Catri enjoyed fishing on the Outer Banks.

Then in 1966, Bob Holland opened a Smith and Holland Surf Shop and his sons, Johnny and Bobby, worked there in the summers. That same year, with Californian Phil Edwards in Virginia Beach for the East Coast Surfing Championships and a *Sports Illustrated* cover photo shoot, Bob Holland took Edwards all the way to Hatteras, checking the surf in each spot. Hobie also made trips to the Outer Banks.

In 1966, the first Nags Head Surfing Tournament was put on by the Outer Banks Surf Club, and the Kahuna Surf Club of Chesapeake was held in big surf generated by Hurricane Faith. In June 1966, the Nags Head Surfing Association was formed in an effort to help the image of surfing and advocate for beach access. There was plenty of work to be done. In August 1967, it was reported that twenty-one people had been fined for "illegal surfing," most of whom were from Virginia.

In 1969, after returning from Hawaii, Bill Frierson moved to Nags Head and made boards right behind his place on the beach. Jimbo Brothers came down, as did Don Bennett, who set up a surfboard factory on the beach across from the Nags Head Pier.

Meanwhile, Smith and Holland Surf Shop in Kill Devil Hills closed when Bob and Pete separated the shops. Then Pete Smith's Surf Shop opened in 1969 at 28th and Pacific.

By the late 1960s, the hot kids surfing there were Bobby Gardner, Christian Binford, Bennett Strickland, Fred Coakley and others.

THE BYPASS AND THE BONNER BRIDGE

Before the bypass, you had to crawl down the beach road to get to the entrance of Cape Hatteras National Seashore. In 1962, the bypass road was built from Kitty Hawk through Nags Head, the same year the Ash Wednesday storm came through.

When the Bonner Bridge over Oregon Inlet was built in 1963, replacing a ferry crossing, all of a sudden surfing Cape Hatteras National Seashore,

Damage to the dune is evident at the Cape Hatteras Lighthouse after the Ash Wednesday storm of 1962. *Aycock Brown Collection, courtesy of the Outer Banks History Center.*

with good surf spots in Rodanthe, Avon, Buxton and Frisco, was much more accessible. Bob Holland and some others started going down to the lighthouse regularly.

Then as now, the journey just to get to the Buxton Lighthouse is a bit of an adventure—rugged, wild, even a little spooky when a storm was coming up and the sun was going down. Driving on a thin strip of road with large ocean dunes on one side and the marshes on the endless sound on the other was nothing like most other beach drives. Days at Hatteras were also long, bright and hot, with impossible mosquitoes, sudden storms and winds that could blow for days.

Hatteras was also magical, seemingly with two oceans, one north of the Cape Point in Buxton and the other on the south side in Avon. If the wind was blowing northeasterly at the lighthouse, then at Avon Pier the winds would be offshore. Surf conditions could change rapidly, and for the better. Seemingly out of nowhere, the surf could be up and breaking nicely.

With the new bridge, Virginia Beach surfers and many others from points farther north started traveling to the Outer Banks on a regular basis for

The Bonner Bridge opened in 1963 as a majestic gateway to Cape Hatteras National Seashore. It closed in 2018 when the new Basnight Bridge opened, named for Marc Basnight, a state senator from Manteo who also was a surfer. *Courtesy of the Outer Banks History Center.*

the warm water and the amazingly consistent surf. Virginia Beach surfers especially did so because they were so close and it was so easy.

The Outer Banks of North Carolina gained a reputation as the East Coast's best surfing, and Buxton, North Carolina, home of the famed lighthouse, became its epicenter. For any Eastern surfer, as word got out, it became a rite of passage to journey either up or down the coast to discover its waves. Surfing on the East Coast found its paradise with the full-on discovery of Cape Hatteras National Seashore.

THE EAST COAST SURFING CHAMPIONSHIPS MOVE TO VIRGINIA BEACH

The East Coast Surfing Championships actually started in Gilgo Beach, New York, on Long Island in 1961, though it appears largely to have been a relatively small, local event. But word got around, and the next year, surfers started coming to the event.

By the early 1960s on Long Island, surfing was becoming entrenched. Reuben Snodgrass opened up a surf shop out of a boathouse around 1960 near Lake Ronkonkoma called Surf Unlimited. John Hannon, having already built several boards from his time on the West Coast in the 1950s, moved back east and opened Hannon Surfboards in Great Neck while working for White Mountain Ski Shop and selling surfboards there. Together, Snodgrass and Hannon were important in getting the contest scene off the ground on Long Island, holding the Lido Beach Surfing Contest on September 9–10, 1961, at the New Town Park in Lido Beach, one of the first modern contests on the East Coast.

On September 8, 1962, the second annual East Coast Surfing Championships were held at Gilgo Beach, Long Island. Sponsored by the Town of Babylon, among the judges were Hannon; Leroy Rapp of Deer Park; Stretch Pohl of Surf City, New Jersey; and Bob Holland of Virginia Beach. Over 210 contestants showed up. Roy Rapp, the chief lifeguard at Gilgo, was also a judge. He noted that form, variety of maneuvers and ability to maintain full control of the board were the criteria for judging. During the competition, 12 surfers battled it out for thirty minutes.

Contestants came from "Virginia, Delaware, Maryland, New Jersey, New York, Connecticut, and Rhode Island, with quite a few visitors from California and Hawaii," according to local press accounts. However, it seems there were no Floridians there for the contest.

The largest out-of-state contingent came from Virginia Beach, with twenty-seven surfers, and the contest was largely a battle between New York and Virginia. George Fisher from Amityville, New York, won the men's event, with Ronnie Mellott in second and Dave Baker in third, both from Virginia Beach. Gary Rice, also from Virginia Beach, won the boys' event.

At the contest, Bob Holland suggested to Hannon moving the contest down to Virginia Beach because of its central location. The water was warmer and easier for the Floridians to reach. Hoppy Swarts, head of the United States Surfing Association (USSA), and Hobie Alter also supported the move.

Facilitating things further was the fact that Virginia Beach businessmen Don Fentress and Webb Brown were friends of Holland's. Fentress was a partner in a prominent insurance firm, which helped bring credibility to the event. Brown and his father ran a clothing business. Fentress and Brown agreed to run the contest under the sponsorship of the Virginia Beach Jaycees, with cooperation from the local surfboard dealers and the Virginia Beach Surfing Club.

In 1963, the Virginia Beach Jaycees sponsored the first ever Virginia Beach Surfing Carnival, under which the East Coast Championships were held. Among the judges were John Hannon from New York; Captain Robert Holland (father of Bob Holland); Dusty Hinnant, the 1930s lifeguard and board pioneer; and Jack "Murph the Surf" Murphy.

Surfers lined up on the beach for the 1965 East Coast Surfing Championships waiting for the horn. *Photo by Buddy Riggs, courtesy of Barbara Eisenberg*

Cars with surfboards on top crowd the parking lot. Then as now, parking was tight. *Photo by Buddy Riggs, courtesy of Barbara Eisenberg*

Organizers of ECSC brought in palm trees for one of the first contests. *Photo by Buddy Riggs, courtesy of Barbara Eisenberg.*

The following month, on September 7–8, 1963, a contest was still held in Gilgo Beach but the torch had been passed to Virginia Beach. According to the program, the surf the day before the contest "was one of the best and biggest days of the season at Gilgo" but dropped to two to three feet shore break for the event. Bill Nugent from California won the men's contest.

On August 29–30, 1964, the second annual Virginia Beach Surfing Carnival was held, under which the East Coast Surfing Championships were held in Virginia Beach for the second year. According to the program, "300 contestants and 2,000 spectators" experienced the event in two-foot surf. It went on to state that "there were several top opposite coast surfers present including Don Hansen, Greg Noll and Dewey Weber."

In 1965, the East Coast Surfing Championships were headlined as such above the "3rd Annual Virginia Beach Surfing Carnival." The Gilgo contest was now called the Gilgo Beach Surfing Championship, held September 12–13, 1964, and also sanctioned by the USSA.

In 1966, after three years as the Virginia Beach Surfing Carnival, that name was phased out and the event was officially known as the East Coast Surfing Championships.

THE VIRGINIA BEACH GUYS COMPETE WELL

From the beginning, the Virginia Beach surfers did well on their home turf (surf), including competition going up against surfers from other points south and north. At the first 1963 ECSC in Virginia Beach, local Ronnie Mellott won the junior men's division over Traylor McQuilkin and Hampton Sewell. In the boys' division, Gary Rice, another Virginia Beach guy, won, followed by Flea Shaw, Chip McQuilkin and Larry Taylor.

However, it was the soon-to-be infamous Jack "Murph the Surf" Murphy from Cocoa Beach who won the senior men's division in a tight battle over Pete Smith. The next year, Murph would be a world-renowned jewel thief known all over the front pages as the Florida playboy champion surfer who stole the Star of India sapphire.

In 1964 at the ECSC, as Murphy would have been planning the New York heist, reigning champ Gary Rice fell to emerging Florida surf star Gary Propper in the junior men's, followed by Jimmy Parnell in third place. John Eakes won the senior men's that year, and Ed McQuilkin won the midgets, followed by John Holland.

Bob Holland would win the first of many East Coast Surfing Championship titles when he won the senior men's in 1965 over John Hannon of New York, then again in 1966 against Mickey Gose of New Jersey and again in 1968 against George Gerlach, also from New Jersey. Holland would go on to win a number of ESA Championships in Hatteras, as well as seven U.S. Surfing Championships. He also served as a judge at major contests and was instrumental in the ECSC moving to Virginia Beach.

In 1967, Bob Holland won his first U.S. Surfing Championship in Huntington Beach, California, and was the first East Coast surfer to win a national title. Later, he won one on the Gulf Coast and then the East Coast, making him one of the only U.S. champs to win on all three coasts. Holland was one of the first East Coast surfers to gain the respect of the Californians and Hawaiians. Holland's two sons, John and Bobby, were also top competitors in their divisions, and later his daughter Honey Holland would win several championships as well.

Californian Corky Carroll won the men's in 1968, but the Otto Seaman Memorial Trophy for overall performance went to John Holland. In 1968, the top three women in the international surfing world were Margo Godfrey (1964 world champion at age fifteen), Linda Benson (1959 U.S. champion at Huntington Beach) and Joyce Hoffman (who went on to earn five world titles through the 1960s and early '70s), who finished first,

A view from the end of the Steel Pier at the East Coast Surfing Championships. *Photo by Buddy Riggs, courtesy of Barbara Eisenberg.*

second and third in Virginia Beach. In 1969, local Freddie Grosskreutz won the men's division over such heralded surfers as Yancy Spencer, Sam Gornto and Warren Bolster.

ECSC was not the only contest held in Virginia Beach in those years. The Tidewater Surf Contest was held in June, the first contest of the year, at the Steel Pier. It was sponsored by the Virginia Beach Surf Club and had more than 100 contestants entered with more than 2,500 spectators. Ronnie Mellott won the men's, Ed McQuilkin won boys' and Norman Grosskruetz won junior men's.

"NEVER USE THE WORD 'SURFBOARD' AGAIN!"

In 1967, Bob White was shaping surfboards in the same storefront where Rosi Surfboards began on 23rd, but he moved the ding repair, shaping and manufacturing to a double garage at the go-cart track on Virginia Beach Boulevard. He hired Bill Frierson, Marty Keesecker and Ronnie Mellott to help out with ding repair and shaping. White took another little storefront down the street and doubled up on his sanding, glassing, shaping and ding repair.

Thanks to the incredible explosion of surfing taking place in the late 1960s, coupled with the early success and reputation that White had developed, some investors got interested, foreseeing a platform from which to launch a venture in the use of fiberglass and plastics, which was an undeveloped market. The investors were Andrew and Morris Fine and Harry Snyder, and they formed U.S. Fiberglass Products Inc. The partners brought in Lou Cady, a Madison Avenue advertising guy by day, who set out to develop and imagine an advertising campaign. "He wanted to get a logo, he wanted to get a whole corporate image going for Bob White Surfboards in general," remembered White. "And I don't know how old *Surfer* is, but I would venture to say that there has never been an eighteen-month advertising campaign to come close to being as effective as his."

Cady would make periodic calls to White from New York. Late one night, Bob White was sleeping when he got a phone call. It was Cady, who asked White a question.

"Who is the greatest wave rider in the world?"

White didn't hesitate. "David Nuuhiwa!"

"Why?"

White recalls answering, incredulous: "'He holds the world's record for hanging ten…*fourteen seconds*. He is the smoothest, most accurate…' and I started going on and on, and finally he waited just long enough to where I really started cranking up and he knew I was awake enough, and he went 'WRONG!'"

"It's not David Nuuhiwa?! Because who is it!?"

"No no no, I'm not even sure it's a human being. I'd like you to put some thought into this thing."

White didn't have to think long. "Well, I can tell you right now for eons, the only other creatures in the world that has ever ridden a wave for pleasure is the dolphin. And there's no question in my mind that he can stand up on his tail and he can ride a wave on his tummy, he can do whatever he wants, he can jump out of the face of the wave if he wants to. I would say by far it is the porpoise. I mean, after all, he doesn't even need a surfboard."

"Great! That's good. Goodnight!"

Some time passed before the next phone call, which again came late at night. "Cady woke me up one night, sat me up in the bed and said, 'Surfboard. What's the definition of *surfboard*?'"

"Ahhhh…jeesh."

White started going through a long explanation. "Well, in the beginning of time, you know, it's this big wooden thing and all this, and you ride it all

Above: M.F. "Babe" Braithwaite varnishes one of his paddleboards on the beach. Babe was a lifeguard at the Marshall's Hotel on 66th Street in Virginia Beach. *Courtesy of Frank Butler.*

Left: Jimmy Hatcher, Clint Walker and Frank Butler hold up paddleboards built by Babe Braithwaite. *Courtesy of Frank Butler.*

In 1962, the East Coast Surfing Championships were held at Gilgo Beach on Long Island. The largest contingent of out-of-state surfers came from Virginia Beach with twenty-seven competitors. *Left to right*: Joe Potter, Mr. Potter, Wayne Morgan, Jimmy Gregory, Nicky Michaels, Butch Maloney, Norman Morse, Jimpe Holland, Tommy Lueke, Ron Smith, Richard Neal and Pete Smith (*standing*). *Courtesy of Pete Smith.*

Phil McAdams announces from the podium at the East Coast Surfing Championships. McAdams was co-chairman of the first ECSC in Virginia Beach, along with Don Fentress. *Photo by Buddy Riggs, courtesy of Barbara Eisenberg.*

Hobie Alter and his wife, Sharon, drove across country in an RV and toured the East Coast looking to promote Hobie Surfboards and help judge surf contests. *Photo by Buddy Riggs, courtesy of Barbara Eisenberg.*

Hobie and Sharon Alter wowed the crowd with their tandem surfing. *Photo by Buddy Riggs, courtesy of Barbara Eisenberg.*

Surfers line up on shore and wait for Hobie Alter (*back to camera*) to give the signal for the competition to begin. *Photo by Buddy Riggs, courtesy of Barbara Eisenberg.*

Phil Edwards, the 1964 world champion, came to Virginia Beach for the 1966 ECSC and was featured the same year on the cover of *Sports Illustrated* surfing the Steel Pier for an article heralding the "East Coast Surfing Boom." *Photo by Buddy Riggs, courtesy of Barbara Eisenberg.*

Greg Noll and Pete Smith at the East Coast Surfing Championships. Noll was a pioneer big wave rider from California, one of the first to ride both Waimea and Pipeline in Hawaii. *Photo by Buddy Riggs, courtesy of Barbara Eisenberg.*

Toes on the nose. *Photo by Buddy Riggs, courtesy of Barbara Eisenberg.*

Judges at ECSC included famed Malibu surf star Mickey Munoz, women's world champion Joyce Hoffman and Hermosa Beach surf star Dewey Weber, along with John Hannon from New York. *Photo by Buddy Riggs, courtesy of Barbara Eisenberg.*

In 1966 and 1967, Jimbo Brothers, a young Virginia Beach surf star in the midgets' division, won ECSC championships with an "exaggerated, powerful style of surfing," wrote the *Virginian Pilot.* "Rather than lay back and wait for the wave to do something, Jimbo attacks the curl with surprising vigor." *Photo by Buddy Riggs, courtesy of Barbara Eisenberg.*

A surfer shoots down the line. *Photo by Buddy Riggs, courtesy of Barbara Eisenberg.*

A crowd watches the surfing action from the beach at ECSC. *Photo by Buddy Riggs, courtesy of Barbara Eisenberg.*

Bob Holland won seven U.S. Surfing championships, including at Huntington Beach; Galveston, Texas; and Cape Hatteras. He also won a dozen ECSC contests in Virginia Beach and numerous ESA titles in Hatteras. *Photo by Buddy Riggs, courtesy of Barbara Eisenberg.*

Sunrise surfers in Virginia Beach. *Photo by Buddy Riggs, courtesy of Pete Smith.*

Girls check their tan lines on the beach at ECSC. *Photo by Buddy Riggs, courtesy of Barbara Eisenberg*

Right: Pete Smith's Surf Shop was an icon in Virginia Beach for many years. *Photo by Buddy Riggs, courtesy of Barbara Eisenberg.*

Below: The VW Microbus was the iconic symbol of 1960s- and 1970s-era hippies and surfers. *Photo by Buddy Riggs, courtesy of Barbara Eisenberg.*

PETE SMITH'S SURF SHOP
28th & PACIFIC VIRGINIA BEACH, VA.

Hatteras Island Surf Shop, founded in 1971 by Barton Decker. *Courtesy of Michael Halminski.*

Whalebone Surf Shop opened in 1975 under the name Resin Craft by Jim Vaughn. Later, the name was changed to Whalebone Junction and then just Whalebone Surf Shop. *Courtesy of Jim Vaughn.*

Surfers line up at the 1982 U.S. Championships in Cape Hatteras. *Author's collection.*

The 1982 U.S. Championships were held at the lighthouse in Cape Hatteras. *Surfing* magazine and Sundek sponsored the contest. *Author's collection.*

17th Street was opened in 1970 by Lee and Harriet Jones. *Courtesy of Harriet Jones and Donna McNelly.*

For many years, Wave Riding Vehicles was located on Norfolk Avenue. *Courtesy of Rick Romano.*

Mickey McCarthy started New Sun Surfboards in the early 1980s on the beach road across from the Nags Head Pier. *Author's collection.*

Lynn Shell at the lighthouse, 1983. *Photo by Mickey McCarthy, courtesy of Lynn Shell.*

Rodanthe Surf Shop was founded in 1989 by Debbie Bell and Randy Hall and later sold to Jason and Lovie Heilig. *Author's collection.*

Cavalier Surf Shop opened in 1962 as a laundromat that also carried surfboards and surf wax and became a full-fledged surf shop in the 1980s under the ownership of Ken and Marty Slayton. *Author's collection.*

Pungo Board House was opened by Dylan and Kari Rogers in 2007. *Author's collection.*

After his time as co-owner of Wave Riding Vehicles, Bill Frierson started a new surfboard-building operation called Frierson Designs. *Author's collection.*

A porpoise jumping out of a wave became the inspiration for the Wave Riding Vehicles logo. *Courtesy of Frank Butler.*

the way and you step on the sand, and it's wood and surf…" and he finally got it down to three words. "I guess the most condensed conceivable one coming from my perspective was 'Wave…Riding…Vehicle.'"

"And Cady said, 'From evermore, forevermore, from the time you open the door tomorrow morning at the factory, forevermore, never use this word 'surfboard' again."

From that point on "Bob White Surfboards" became "Bob White/Wave Riding Vehicles."

Again, some time passed before White got another phone call.

"Oh, by the way," Cady was on the line asking, "what is the greatest single objective of riding a wave? I've been reading the magazines, and I have not figured out what the single objective is in riding a wave."

"Well, I guess really it would be to get to the curl," White said. "You're on the shoulder and you cut back to get to that tube, and if you're way back deep and you're in the white water and you're trying to push on out…I guess it's to get to the tube…to be tubed is the greatest single objective!"

Cady took the information and with a graphic artist named John Nunnman came up with the breaking wave of the five dolphins. With the new name and logo, the advertising campaign in *Surfer* commenced in the spring of 1968. The first ad was a two-page centerspread called "Riderdore."

The iconic WRV logo was inspired by the curling porpoises that were frequently found in the waters of Virginia Beach. *Author's collection.*

Bob White/Wave Riding Vehicles. *Author's collection.*

To help launch the campaign, they sold a poster through the mail for twenty-five cents. Thousands of requests came in from places like Nova Scotia, Puerto Rico and all up and down the East Coast, plus California, Hawaii and even Germany.

Wave Riding Vehicles was also doing some unusual marketing for a surf shop. One tactic was selling surfboards into the military procurement system. The other was establishing accounts with Sears department store on the East Coast and Puerto Rico.

Problems arose with the mass merchandising of the fragile surfboards. "The general merchandiser does not know how to handle delicate commodities," said White. "I had to go to the dealerships and replace damaged boards that I knew were not our fault."

The shop's reputation spread until one day the U.S. Department of Commerce called and said that WRV had been recommended as the East Coast surfboard manufacturer to represent the product at a big expo in Japan. White made three pure white boards and shipped them.

"Right in the middle, we had our three pure white boards sitting up on these pedestals, and all around them are these great big California boards with all these colors, and the white boards just stood out and made the rest all just look like background."

All along, White experimented with different shapes. His often controversial—but in many ways ahead of their time—surfboard designs inspired much comment, but he foresaw many of the design changes to come. While everybody came out with stuff like the step deck, the feather, the this or that, White started running ads introducing his new "Little Diminutive

By April 1968, *Surfing* magazine reported a "Surfboard Revolution Going On," followed in December by an editorial titled "The Death of the Longboard" that described a funeral for one million obsolete surfboards. All of a sudden, boards got shorter by a foot and weird things started happening. *Photo by Buddy Riggs, courtesy of Barbara Eisenberg.*

Baby Tear Drops" that were just coming out. Along with the innovations came a little mysticism.

Virginia Beach already had a well-established but still evolving manufacturing niche. Al Roper had sold his interest to Bob White on Rosi Surfboards and moved to California to shape for Hobie. In the "goo" early on, you had Bill Frierson, Marty Keesecker, Mike Doyle and Ronnie Mellott shaping for WRV and other new ventures.

But times were changing, and longboards were being replaced by shorter boards. Two feet were being chopped off, and new shapes were being introduced. One result of the shortboard revolution was that it hurt the surf industry because 1) it made it harder to surf and 2) it killed the shops that had stocked up on longboards that no one now wanted. When Johnny Fain from Malibu came out with his shortboards, "surfing stopped," recalled Renny Koseff from Long Beach Island, New Jersey. All of a sudden, longboards were out and no one wanted them any longer. Then the design race was on for the perfect shortboard.

Nobody knew for sure what was going to happen next. Surfboards were evolving faster during that period of time than at any other in the history of the sport. Every sixty days, *Surfer* magazine came out with a whole new thing. The shortboard revolution inspired a burst of surfboard manufacturing in Virginia Beach.

AMERICA SURFBOARDS, EASTSIDE, WEST WIND, BOARDS BY DON BENNETT AND MEDIUM BETWEEN MAN AND WAVE

By 1966, Smith and Holland Surf Shop was doing a good business, carrying a "stoking selection" of Kanvas by Katin and Birdwell Beach Britches, along with Aloha and Rincon racks, Lunada Bay wetsuits and skateboards. In 1966, the store sold about six hundred Hobies—the "Cadillacs of the surfing world"—and was responsible for 10 percent of Hobie's worldwide business.

"Now 70 percent of our boards go to the East Coast shops," Hobie told *Sports Illustrated*. "Smith and Holland, our biggest individual Eastern dealer, along with Reitman's Manatee Sea shops in Jersey and Emilio's on Long Island all outsell our Hawaiian outlet."

"Both Smith and Holland are enthusiastic," the article continued. "They run their shop wearing shorts and breakaway sneakers and when the surf is up they march right out and reopen later when the waters calm down."

Along with the political battles and a growing contest circuit of the mid- to late 1960s, the East Coast was sprouting a burgeoning infrastructure of surfboard builders and manufacturers, and Virginia Beach had a large presence. Many of the West Coast and Australian boards were being ridden on the East Coast, including the Hobie "Gary Propper Model," the Australian V-Bottom, the Con Butterfly series ridden by Claude Codgen and Bruce Valluzzi and Weber boards by Mike Tabeling.

Virginia Beach already had a well-established but still evolving manufacturing presence. Then in 1968, the shortboard revolution inspired a burst of surfboard manufacturing in the area. On the heels of Wave Riding Vehicles getting up and running, there was a flurry of surfboard- building activity going on all over Virginia Beach, with a lot of new surf shops opening up. Plus, a new industry created itself in all the mayhem: ding repair. M and M Ding Repair, which stood for McQuilkin and Myers, later became M&L Ding Repair (new partner unknown).

Bill Frierson moved from California to Virginia Beach with his family in 1965. He quickly got on Pete Smith's Hobie team and soon after that started learning to make surfboards. Frierson got his first start shaping boards working with Bob White, doing ding repair and helping build boards.

Meanwhile, surf shops and outlets selling boards kept cropping up. Coaches Sporting Goods, owned by Fred Isaacs, was among the first in Virginia Beach to sell popout surfboards. In 1964, Virginia Beach Hardware, on the corner of Virginia Beach Boulevard and Baltic Avenue, sold Hansen Surfboards. Also in 1964, Virginia Surf Shoppe ran an ad in the ECSC program.

In 1965, Butch Maloney opened Butch's Surf Shop on 19th Street and sold Hap Jacob Surfboards. Also in 1965, Bahia Surfboards opened on Atlantic Avenue, selling Webers and skimboards. Al Sneblin opened up Al's Surf Shop with two locations, one in 1966 on 19th and Atlantic and another in 1967 located right under the Steel Pier. He opened a shop in Nags Head also, across from E. Blackman Street, north of the pier. Jimbo Brothers was a team rider. In 1967–68, Virginia Beach Surf Shop was run by Jim Callerhan and Jett Colanna.

In 1967, Harris Pulley opened Harris Surf Shop and not long after changed the name to Harris Surf and Ski in Virginia Beach. He later opened one in Kill Devil Hills as well as other locations around Tidewater, including one at Military Circle and another on Granby Street.

Norfolk had other outlets selling surfboards. At the Martens and Davis Diving and Surfboard Shop at 5107 Colley Avenue near Old Dominion

College (ODC), you could buy Con and Yater boards. The Sportsman Shop on Plume Street also sold boards starting in 1964. And in 1965, Atlantic Paint and Plastic Co., on Hampton Boulevard also near ODC, sold "Custom Made Surfboards," as well as fiberglass materials and Walker blanks.

Along came America Surfboards from about 1968 to 1971, with a patriotic yet rogue reputation. It tested the limits not only in surfing but also in society's tolerance for its sometimes risqué boards. It was started by Viv Hodgson and run by Al Roper, who brought his Hobie experience back from California to help create a surfboard manufacturing operation, along with Bill Frierson, Ronnie Mellott and Robert Myers. Chip McQuilkin, a surfer and artist, came up with the logo. With demand so high immediately, Roper brought in Terry Martin, a Hobie shaper from California, to help keep up. America was just starting up but was daring, on the cutting edge and selling boards like crazy. For a brief time, America Surfboards also had a shop in Frisco.

Meanwhile, Mellott, Frierson and Al Sneblin started shaping for a shop called Eastside. Then Don Bennett came up from the Outer Banks, and West Wind made its presence. All of these manufacturers were located around 19th and Cypress Avenues, where WRV is today. Some of the shapers migrated between all the surfboard labels before Bennett went back to the Outer Banks and produced Surfboards by Don. After a few years, Bob White left WRV, and he went on to do surfboards under the name Medium Between Man and Wave, the X-Series and the Real McCoy.

MEET DICK CATRI AND JACK "MURPH THE SURF" MURPHY

In the midst of what was happening in Virginia Beach and on the Outer Banks, the rise of surfing was just as enthusiastic up and down the East Coast. Surfing was cool and fun, and if you were lucky enough to be a part of it, you were lucky, because the rest of America was listening to the Beach Boys and watching beach party movies, and they wanted to be a part of it.

Surfing had a large impact on culture and fashion all over America. There were also some real-life colorful characters and interesting personalities in the world of surfing, with names like Hobie, Dewey and Corky from the West Coast and Dick Catri and Jack "Murph the Surf" Murphy from Florida. All made their mark and had a lasting effect in Virginia Beach at the East Coast Surfing Championships.

Not surprisingly, due partly to its natural advantages in terms of the weather, population and pier, Cocoa Beach, Florida, emerged as a surf center during the late '50s and early '60s. The missile race was starting to take hold, there were thousands of servicemen at Patrick Air Force Base and there were thousands of engineers working at Cape Canaveral. Astronauts were being shot into orbit. Cocoa Beach even had its own TV sitcom, *I Dream of Jeannie*.

Dick Catri and Jack Murphy met and became friends and cohorts, going on surfing adventures up and down the coast of Florida and up to Nags Head and Virginia Beach, either separately or together. Catri enjoyed fishing, so he was drawn to Hatteras, and Murphy was a competitor and judge in 1963 at the Virginia Beach Surfing Carnival, now known as the East Coast Surfing Championships. Both were big guys with magnetic personalities, and they weren't afraid to get in trouble. Murphy in particular would find more than his share.

Murphy had acquired the moniker "Murph the Surf" from a group of Miami lifeguards, and by this time, he had won the major Florida contests. In 1963, he won the senior men's division at the Virginia Beach Surfing Carnival, also known as the East Coast Surfing Championships. He owned Murph's Surf Shop, but more than that, he was known as a bit of a gifted Renaissance man. He was accomplished on violin during his youth in Pittsburgh, and after time in California, he migrated to Florida, where he performed diving exhibitions and made hats out of palm fronds for tourists.

Catri, meanwhile, left in 1960 for Hawaii, where he remained for four years. Back in Florida, Murphy hooked up with Alan Kuhn, a surfer and jewel thief who spent his time motoring up and down the Indian River scoping the luxurious homes and the jewelry contained in them. Typically, Murphy and Kuhn docked their speedboat in front of the waterfront estates and expertly made their way inside the homes, deactivating not just the indoor security systems but those in the yard as well. As portrayed in the movie *Murph the Surf*, it was with a deft touch that they stole the jewelry from homes and then fenced them, leaving not a trace of evidence. But suspicions arose about how a couple of ne'er-do-well beach bums enjoyed a lifestyle of expensive cars, fast boats and nice homes.

With the success of these relatively small heists, they hungered for something bigger, something that would set them up for life. Their plan: to steal the Star of India, the largest sapphire in the world, from the Museum of Natural History in New York City.

When they successfully made the hit on October 29, 1964, not only was it the biggest jewel heist in history, but it also had the added glamour and intrigue of a couple of charismatic beach bums—one a surfing champion. The headlines were huge. What followed was a high-pressure investigation of Murphy. (A major motion picture about the heist was released in 1975 called *Live a Little, Steal a Lot*, starring Robert Conrad as Allen Kuhn and Don Stroud as Murphy. It was later reissued as *Murph the Surf*.)

Although local legend had it that the Star of India sapphire was hidden in a bag on the ocean floor at the end of the Cocoa Beach pier, the jewel was reportedly "found" in a Miami bus station locker—in exchange for a three-year prison sentence at Riker's Island in New York for both Kuhn and Murphy. By January 1967, Murphy was released from prison, but not for long.

The same year, Murphy was involved in the so-called Whiskey Creek Murders, bringing more sensational headlines, and was sentenced to life in prison. After turning to God and demonstrating good works, in 1986 he was released to work in prison ministry.

FLORIDA'S RISING SURF STARS MAKE THEIR PRESENCE KNOWN

Dick Catri left Florida in 1960 for Hawaii, where he remained for four years. He became the first Florida surfer to tackle the big waves of the North Shore. With that came cameos in surf movies by Bud Browne, Dale Dobson and Bruce Brown. He was also the aquatic director of *Ride the Wild Surf* and appeared on the cover of a surf album by Dick Dale and the DelTones. He met up with other East Coasters making early trips to the islands. Among them were Shelley Stevens of New York, Mickey Gose of New Jersey, Jim Phillips of Delaware and Butch Maloney of Virginia Beach.

In 1965, Catri returned from his years in Hawaii and opened Satellite Surf Shop. With Murphy in jail for the jewel theft, Catri—fresh from Hawaii and all the success and lore that brought—became a dominant player in the Florida surf scene. For the fledgling Grand Prix surfing contest circuit that was now happening, he organized powerful surf teams and toured the East Coast surf towns, coming to Virginia Beach every year for the East Coast Surfing Championships. The surf crew could be found by looking no farther than Cocoa Beach High School. Roaming the halls there were Gary Propper, Claude Codgen and Bruce Valluzzi.

Propper, along with Codgen, Valluzzi and Mike Tabeling, ushered in the era of the surf star. Originally from Miami, Gary Propper learned to surf on a six-foot Phil Edwards and moved to Cocoa Beach at age twelve in 1964. In 1966, he beat famed California surfer Dewey Weber in Virginia Beach at the East Coast Surfing Championships.

Propper became the first big East Coast surf star of the 1960s and the first East Coaster to have his own line of boards. The Gary Propper by Hobie became Hobie's best-selling model, with over three thousand sold in one year, half of Hobie's overall sales. Propper in his later career would become a talent agent for Carrot Top, the comedian, along with others, but he really hit the big time when he optioned the rights to *Teenage Mutant Ninja Turtles*, the Saturday morning cartoon, from which he became a multimillionaire.

Codgen was a nose-rider extraordinaire who exuded style and grace. In 1966, he became the number-one East Coast junior. That year, he went to the World Contest in San Diego, where Con Surfboards recruited him to surf for them. In 1967, he won the East Coast Surfing Championships in Virginia Beach and was invited to the Duke contest in Hawaii. He then went to Peru with Catri. In 1966, he introduced his Claude Codgen signature model called CC Rider, which he produced until 1969.

Mike Tabeling, meanwhile, surfed for Weber. Tabeling was Mr. Energy, an excellent paddler who could ride absolutely anything. When he was out, no one would catch more waves. Energy poured out of his body as he came off the bottom turn, slapped the lip and then did a strong roundhouse cutback.

Valluzzi distinguished himself on big waves in Hawaii and elsewhere and was also the East Coast's chronicler, writing articles and offering photos for the surf mags.

AT FIFTEEN, MIMI MUNRO RETIRES AS EAST COAST CHAMPION

Mimi Munro won the ECSC girls' division in both 1965 and 1966. She was an eleven-year-old girl from Ormond Beach, Florida, just north of Daytona, in 1963 when she began surfing. The next year, she won the Florida State Surfing Championships. She surfed for Dick Catri's powerful Surfboards Hawaii team on the Grand Prix contest circuit, winding up in Virginia Beach for ECSC during its heyday. She wowed the crowds with her ability to walk the board and hang ten in spectacular fashion. Then at age fifteen, she retired from competitive surfing.

On the East Coast, a popular place for surfers looking for an education was Brevard Community College (now Eastern Florida State College) on

Mimi Munro from Ormond Beach, Florida, won the women's ECSC championship in Virginia Beach. *Photo by Buddy Riggs, courtesy of Barbara Eisenberg.*

the central Florida coast. The allure of warm water near Cocoa Beach was enticing. All of a sudden, people were going away to community college in Florida and, from there, hopping over to Puerto Rico for the Christmas holiday. Many also moved there without going to college, spending the winter there surfing. The Crescent Beach Apartments in Cocoa Beach was where a lot of the surfers lived, including Gary Propper, Warren Bolster and Bill Bringhurst, along with Jimbo Brothers and Fred Grosskreutz from Virginia Beach. Mike Tabeling lived at the next apartment house.

Farther south, Sebastian Inlet began getting a reputation for above-average surf. Some were even comparing it to Hatteras. In 1969, a jetty was built there that formed a wave on the north side that opened up a whole new world of surfing. Predictably, battles erupted with the fishermen over who had access to the waters.

Dick Catri addressed the county commission and the inlet commission. After the state acquired the property, he went to Tallahassee to argue the case before the state authorities on the basis of equal access. Negotiations with the State Parks Department produced a designated surfing beach extending six hundred feet from the jetty.

As the 1960s were coming to a close, Sebastian Inlet became a major new surf spot, with Larry Pope and Alan Margolis shooting photos for *Surfer* and other magazines. Jim Cartland, Jeff Crawford and Greg Loehr were down for frequent photo sessions, along with Tabeling. It got them in the magazines with sizable Florida surf.

However, Cape Hatteras maintained its allure and reputation as the most consistent and magical surf spot on the East Coast.

Chapter 3

The '60s

The Cult of Surf Worship

Bruce Brown was a Californian who since 1958 had made several surf movies, including *Slippery When Wet*, *Barefoot Adventure* and *Waterlogged*. In 1963, he produced his most successful project ever: *The Endless Summer*. Brown, Mike Hynson and Robert August traveled around the world, searching for the "perfect wave."

After premiering the movie in California in late June, Brown and his wife, Patricia, along with Phil Edwards, Corky Carroll, Joey Cabell, Hobie Alter and Mike Hynson, left California in an RV and headed to New York to perform surf demonstrations and to premiere the film along the East Coast.

They took the show to Chaminade High School in Hempstead, Long Island, on June 30, 1964, and Asbury Park Convention Center two days later. Down the coast it went, and when it finally reached Daytona, it played the Peabody Auditorium to a packed house of hundreds of stoked kids. They got to Cocoa Beach on July 15.

By the summer of 1964, surfing on the East Coast had reached "crazed proportions" and, according to newspaper accounts, was the fastest-growing sport in the world. When the caravan reached Virginia Beach on July 7, fresh from Ocean City, Maryland, one thousand people "stretched dozens deep for several blocks" came out to watch the surfing demonstration at the Steel Pier.

What they saw was tandem surfing by Hobie and his wife. They saw Phil Edwards, recently voted the "World's Best Surfer" by *Surfer* magazine, ride the nose and cut across the wave. They saw Pacific Coast Junior Champion

Corky Carroll and *Endless Summer* star Mike Hynson "kneel, squat, ride backwards, and while parallel on one wave, accomplish a transfer that had both ending on one surfboard." Later, they saw Hobie give a free boarding demonstration, where he rode on the wake of a boat.

That night, Bruce Brown didn't just play the movie; he personally narrated the film before a packed house at the Virginia Beach Dome. The film may not have even had a soundtrack yet. After it finally was released after full production, the movie would have a profound effect on the image of surfing worldwide, capturing crowds with its "around-the-world" adventure told with gentle humor.

The movie went through final production in late 1965, and Brown tried to interest Hollywood to back it, but without success. To prove a point, during the winter of 1966, Brown reportedly took the film to Wichita, Kansas, where it played to sold-out audiences. Soon after, he opened it in Boston, Washington and other major cities. It premiered in New York at Kipps Bay Movie Theater and was mobbed.

Later that summer, Greg Noll, another Hawaiian big wave pioneer, toured the East Coast, giving his own surf demonstrations and showing the film *Let There Be Surf* by Jim Freeman. Noll first surfed Hawaii in the late 1950s with a style that earned him the nickname the "Bull."

Surf movies became the hot ticket in town through the mid- and late '60s. "You never had to worry about filling the house," said Virginia Beach shaper/surfer Bob White. "Everybody wanted to see a surf movie. There were plenty of surfers to go around and not enough movies to go around then."

It also inspired a legion of eastern filmmakers with their own dreams of capturing the spirit of surfing. Bill Yerkes, a film school graduate, produced *How the East Was Won* and others. Mickey Gose went to Hawaii in 1964 to shoot films for his Gross Gose Flix, Inc. Dan Herlihy from Delaware produced films from his travels to Puerto Rico in the mid-1960s.

THE CULT OF SURF WORSHIP

As the 1960s wore on, the innocent image that had permeated surfing gave way as the Beatles and Rolling Stones landed in America and war raged in Vietnam. As the psychedelic era took hold and great societal upheaval continued, so, too, did the surfing image evolve from the beach bum stereotype. It became surfer as outlaw.

In the summer of 1965, the *New York Times* reported the rise of the "cult of surf worship" that was beginning to "take on the proportions of a major fad." The United States Surfing Association (USSA) was projecting there to be several million surfers in the United States, "and the number has been almost doubling annually."

The *Times* reported:

> *In California there are two types of surf worshippers. One consists of the beach bum set—men and women who all but live on the beach and make no attempt to earn a regular living.*
>
> *Though they may occasionally foment fights or even modest riots, the full-time surfers normally tend to keep to themselves....In habits and appearance these surfers are not unlike the roving motorcycle clubs, with rough attire, beards, and exotic sexual customs.*

The second group was more tame, consisting mainly of high school and college kids who "still manage to spend at least a few hours a day at the beach."

Surfing wasn't confined to coastal areas, either. Grand Haven, Michigan, and other Great Lakes localities boasted a surfing culture in fresh-water surf without the tidal flow. They also used boats and other novel means to ride like surfers.

> *In lake areas wake surfing, in which surfers ride their boards in the wake of motorboats has taken hold. In cities millions of children have become devotees of sidewalk surfing—riding small skateboards. Surfing festivals are proliferating in the East, too, on Long Island, parts of Cape Cod and in Florida.*
>
> *Surfing associations have been trying this year to improve the image of the surfer by steering the hardcore beach bums away from surfing competitions and festivals.*

In Virginia Beach, there were similar "problems." The *Virginia Beach Beacon* noted as much in an editorial titled "Give Surfing a Good Name." "Unfortunately, the sport has acquired a certain aura generated by some adherents who perhaps released a few inhibitions that should have stayed pent-up. To some people, the surfing fraternity has come to be regarded as an undesirable cult."

In 1965, the Norfolk *Virginian-Pilot* noted that the advent of surfing had touched off a "social revolution in taste, in sport, and in occupation. There are now six local shops selling the boards."

There were also unintended side effects, including injuries and liabilities, theft and even changes to football practice. "Local ordinances have been passed restricting the surfing areas because of the dangers to swimmers from runaway boards. Each board now has a number embedded into its surface because of the theft problem, and early football practice has been hard hit because most local youngsters would rather ride the breakers than scrimmage."

The editorial fretted over the consequences. "Surfing often seems to be the major concern of today's youth. They absorb every bit of information on it they can and support anything pertaining to surfing."

One unmistakable trait of the surfer was the style of dress, emulated by "hodads" and inlanders alike. "There's blazing wild fashion on the measly 500-foot strip of surfing beach," reported the *Virginian-Pilot* in 1966. "No doubt about it, here the surfers are the fashion catalysts for the Pepsi generation. Surfing attire is wildly mad."

A new style of surf trunks called "jams" was replacing the traditional surf baggies. Jams were loose-fitting floral trunks designed by Dave Rochlen, one of the first California surfers to move to Hawaii. "Rochlen took the comfort of sleeping pajamas ('Jams' from the word pajamas) then colored them with bright hues of the 50th state," reported the *Pilot*.

"You're out on your board all day, man, you gotta have comfort," explained one surfer.

Likewise for the girls, the *Pilot* reported that long, stringy, sun-bleached hair was a status symbol, along with the floral beach wear. The *Pilot* posed the question, "Whatever became of bathing caps?"

"Squaresville," came the answer.

"SURFING IS A THING NOW"

The year 1966 was big for eastern surfing. It was the year that the East Coast sent a contingent to the World Surfing Championships in San Diego, *Sports Illustrated* featured Virginia Beach surfing on its cover and East beat West at the East Coast Surfing Championships. It's the year Smith and Holland opened a shop in Kill Devil Hills while Pete continued to run the shop in Virginia Beach, selling Hobie Alter Surfboards and Kavas by Katin.

In July that year, *Sports Illustrated* hit the stands with the cover story "Surfing's East Coast Boom: Top Stylist Phil Edwards Rides at Virginia Beach." The story reported:

Surfing has boomed because it is the quickest-stoking sport ever. While it often takes several lessons and some cold practice before one can learn to enjoy skiing, the first ride standing up on a surfboard—no matter how sloppily—is a wild, winging sensation.

Slicing along the front of a wave evokes a feeling of rising from the sea to conquer the world. The water is alive with sparkle, and the surfboard makes a hissing sound like a thousand yards of tearing silk. The board coasts along about 15–20 miles an hour but the boil of the water makes it feel like 180.

A few weeks earlier, California surf star Phil Edwards had come to town for the story, staying with Bob Holland. The kids around the Steel Pier were "buzzing," wrote the *Pilot*. "Know who that is? That's Phil *Edwards*, that's who that is!"

Holland took Edwards on a true surf safari to the Outer Banks, stopping at the piers and breaks along the way looking for waves, but without significant success. They came back, and Edwards did the photo shoot at the Steel Pier.

About 150 fans watched with "unabashed admiration" as Edwards demonstrated the famous "hot dogging" style he helped pioneer. "Wow, did you see that!" kids were overheard saying on the beach. "Look at that one-stroke start!"

The article continued:

While most people were looking the other way, surfing has become perhaps the fastest growing sport along the more than 1500 miles of Eastern seacoast and inlets. There are more than 50,000 Eastern surfers, by ragged estimate, and Lord knows how many more who carry surfboards atop their cars as prestige props.

At Virginia Beach, on a perfect day, the surfing zone is packed with little ones just this side of puberty. Half of them are in the water by the Steel Pier, straddling their boards, waiting for the best waves to come curling in; the other half are standing in struck poses on the beach with boards under their arms waiting for an opening.

There are, as you read this, uncounted thousands of people standing on grounded surfboards with ripples lapping up around their ankles—looking rapturous. Surfing is a thing now. It is here.

With all this energy, a proliferation of surf mags hit the newsstands, all vying for the surf-starved reader. *Surfer* remained the Bible, but in 1964, a

Phil Edwards, the 1964 world champ, surfing at the Steel Pier. Edwards appeared on the cover of *Sports Illustrated* celebrating the "East Coast Surf Boom." *Photo by Buddy Riggs, courtesy of Barbara Eisenberg.*

Bob Holland with surfboards in car, ready to go. *Courtesy of Pete Smith.*

new magazine out of California called *International Surfing*, later to become *Surfing*, was started by John Peterson.

And the East Coast joined the fray. In 1965, *Atlantic Surfing* was started by a man named Paul Chapey in Brooklyn, New York. The next year, two new East Coast magazines would start up: *Surfing East*, founded by Richard S. Van Winkle out of Ridgewood, New Jersey, as part of the Surfing East Association (SEA); and *Competition Surf*, founded by James F. Joiner of Plainview, New York. *Wave Rider* was a Florida-based magazine that started in the 1970s.

"A HOT RIVALRY WAS BREWING"

As on the West Coast, a thriving competitive circuit was brewing in the East, and by the summer of 1966, a hot rivalry was developing between Dewey Weber and Gary Propper. Weber, of course, was the hot board walker and board manufacturer from Hermosa Beach, California. Propper, a Floridian, was "probably the most exciting East Coast surfer today," according to the surfing press. He was the first surf star from the East.

The circuit, known as the Grand Prix of Surfing, was sponsored by *Surfing East* magazine and its publisher, Dick Van Winkle, who also formed the Surfing East Association. The circuit began in 1964 and included ten events from Cape Cod to Cocoa Beach. The big events came at the end of the summer, with the Gilgo, Seaside Heights, Virginia Beach and Cocoa Beach contests clustered over a two-week period leading up to Labor Day.

At Seaside Heights, the Atlantic States Surfing Contest, held August 25–26, was "quite an event." Hurricane Faith had started sending swells, and the several hundred contestants, including a strong group from the West Coast, went head to head in a showdown between East and West.

As a crowd of five thousand watched the three- to five-foot swell roll in, *Surfing East* wrote that they "saw the finest surfing Seaside Heights ever witnessed." Bob Holland won the senior men's division, and Mimi Munro won the girls' event. But Dewey Weber and Gary Propper were pitted for the first time in competition, and all eyes were glued.

The seven-man final included four Californians and three East Coasters. Propper continually found himself locked between the West Coasters, making it difficult to get waves, according to press accounts. Meanwhile, Weber was doing "quick machine gun steps to the nose, radical cutbacks, and powerful kick-outs." Weber won that contest; Propper came in fourth.

Two days later, the East Coast Surfing Championships were on for Virginia Beach. The big news was that the top five male and top two female surfers would be sent to the third World Surfing Championships, to be held October 1–2 in San Diego.

Surfing East magazine reported that Hurricane Faith was still kicking up waves, and over fifteen thousand people were reported to turn out during the two-day event to watch the more than four hundred contestants compete in sixteen events in a three- to six-foot swell with light offshore winds. Among the judges were Hobie Alter, Reynolds Yater, Dewey Weber and Greg Noll.

On the top end of the scale, Bob Holland defended his crown as the top surfer over thirty on the East Coast, with Mickey Gose of New Jersey in second and John Hannon of Long Island in third.

Propper, meanwhile, took the men's competition in a tight battle over teammate Bruce Valluzzi. But it was at the West Coast Open event that Propper would match up with Weber for the showdown.

With the crowd cheering on the East Coast favorite, Propper came through with "one of the most all-time, out-of-sight, unreal, are you ready for this rides," putting the pressure on Weber and the others. Weber did his best moves but lost his board several times. Meanwhile, Bob Lonardo performed a classic nose ride straight to the beach to take second. Weber came in third. Propper had won it!

Robert Myers and Gary Rice catch a wave. *Photo by Buddy Riggs, courtesy of Barbara Eisenberg.*

Above: Floridian Gary Propper beat famed California surfer Dewey Weber at the 1966 East Coast Surfing Championships in Virginia Beach. *Photo by Buddy Riggs, courtesy of Barbara Eisenberg.*

Left: Floridians came to ECSC and took home most, but not all, of the trophies. *Photo by Buddy Riggs, courtesy of Barbara Eisenberg.*

The next issue of *Surfer* displayed the headline never before seen: "East Beats West," noting that Propper served notice that the East Coast was "coming of age in surfdom's competition warfare."

"Undoubtedly the best and most interesting surfing meet yet produced on Eastern shores," reported *Competition Surf*. Meanwhile, all seven berths to the World Surfing Championships went to Floridians, including Gary Propper, Tom McRoberts, Mike Tabeling, Bruce Valluzzi and Fletcher Sharp. Mimi Munro and Cathy LaCroix made it for the girls.

The remaining six places were decided at the final East Coast event at Gilgo Beach on September 17–18, where over 380 contestants vied. After the early rounds, the surf dropped, and the semifinals and finals were postponed until the next weekend. With Larry Minniard, Bruce Clelland and Renee Eisler unable to return, they were awarded berths based on their scores in the preliminaries.

Meanwhile, three spots remained, with Floridian Claude Codgen and New Yorker John Schneller taking the first two spots with their respective wins. It came down to a surf-off between the two second-place finishers, Johnny Holland of Virginia Beach and Eric Eastman of New York, to decide the last berth.

The surf was poor, and the event was decided on a best three out of four waves through fifteen minutes. Each rode the required number. Holland worked a beautiful nose ride while also executing "finely tuned" nose pullouts. Eastman put on a good show, but the day was Holland's, who won the event and the last ticket to San Diego. Dick Catri went as coach and Bob Holland as judge.

The 1966 East Coast contest season, which included a record number of contests, demonstrated an extraordinary level of competition, particularly from the Floridians. However, there were growing pains. There was no sanctioning body, rules at each contest were different, standards of judging varied and a certain frustration was prevalent.

CIVIC POLITICS INVADES SURFING

Back home, civic politics invaded the free-spirited world of surfing, which was now the subject of city hall discussions and lead editorials decrying "the many surfing problems at Virginia Beach." The problem, quite simply, was that in a city where existed the largest Hobie and Weber dealers in the world, there was literally the smallest surfing area in the world—"a typical Eastern

It's no surprise that the Virginia Beach Surf Club logo on your jacket was a major status symbol. More importantly, the VBSC worked to improve the image of surfing. *Courtesy of Pete Smith.*

Syndrome." The cruel irony was that Virginia Beach held a spot in the *Guinness Book of World Records* as the "largest resort city in the world," with twenty-eight miles of beaches. Yet there was just over one hundred yards of surfing beach; the rest was reserved for the paying tourist trade, along with territorial fishermen.

The Virginia Beach Surfing Club was formed in June 1963, and at that time there were about 250 surfers in Virginia Beach. In July 1963, the club lobbied city council successfully to set aside the first official surfing beach. The result was 375 feet beginning 200 feet north of the Steel Pier. At the time, it was adequate.

But by 1964, as crowding boomed and solutions seemed few, rumors persisted of an effort to have surfing banned outright. Again, the Virginia Beach Surfing Club went before the council. "There has been vigorous demand that additional surfing areas be opened up, especially in North Virginia Beach, and equally vigorous opposition," the *Pilot* reported.

With as many as two thousand surfers at the beach on a given week, all sporting ten-foot boards with no leashes and angling for a spot next to the pier, surfers were suffocating in the lineup and, worse, getting hit. "From about 50 feet out on the water looking in, one has the scary sensation of getting ready to surf down the main stairway of Grand Central Station into the 5:15 rush hour crowd," reported *Sports Illustrated*. "Someone is always getting zonked with a board."

"A runaway board carried shoreward by a wave or a swell," reported the *Pilot*, "can easily lay open a scalp or fracture a nose, and many of them have done so."

Because the hotels and motels catered to immediate beach access for paying customers, there was little thought of imposing surfing beaches there. Meanwhile, fishermen on the Steel Pier weren't pleased either. Crossing boundaries meant breaking the law.

In 1965, the City of Virginia Beach began strict enforcement of surfing laws, backed by the threat of jail for surfing too close to the pier. That year,

Surfing was a point of controversy in the community, with fishermen, hotel owners, tourists and the city all pitted against surfing for economic and safety reasons. *Photo by Buddy Riggs, courtesy of Barbara Eisenberg.*

on the first day of enforcement in mid-May, sixty people were arrested for "unlawful surfing."

The surfing problem was addressed in a local 1965 editorial that accurately described the dilemma:

> *The city is in the precarious position of owing a certain responsibility to the surfers, the swimmers and the hotel/motel owners.*
>
> *…Surfing is growing by leaps and bounds, and this resort city is fast becoming known as the leading surfing spot on the East Coast.*
>
> *We must keep surfing in its proper perspective but we cannot ignore it. It's here to stay and is going to become more prevalent as the months go by. We also cannot overlook the financial benefits that might be derived from this sport. Surfing has become big business.*

The Outer Banks of North Carolina, which prided itself on its world-class fishing, also confronted surfing. Villages on the national seashore were

Above: Surfers were the intruders around fishing piers, and fishermen were not fond of surfers. *Courtesy of the Outer Banks History Center.*

Left: Surfers weren't just up against town elders and fishermen; they were sometimes up against the fish, which included this shark caught off Jennette's Pier. *Courtesy of the Outer Banks History Center.*

fishing towns first, and the local businesses largely catered to fishermen as well as summer beach vacationers.

Surfers were the intruders around the fishing piers and along tourist beaches. Pier owners did not like surfers, and the law was that surfers had to stay 350 feet from the piers. Fortunately, with long stretches of beaches, there was room to spread out, even if not at the best spots. And the Buxton Lighthouse surfing area kept conflicts to a minimum, as it got the best surf and fishermen had plenty of room to fish elsewhere.

Nags Head was world famous for fishing, which was a big business, but as surfing grew in popularity and out-of-town surfers started coming in, problems did arise with the fishermen. With conflict prevalent, there were pleas to city hall on both sides to restrict or allow surfing by the pier. In the mid-1960s, local surfers started a group called the Nags Head Surf Club.

THE REST OF THE EAST COAST FIGHTS THE SAME BATTLES

In Rhode Island, surfing laws dating to 1956 required that "every surfer shall be a qualified swimmer and shall present on demand a swimmers card." On Long Island, for a time surfing was banned everywhere except for Gilgo Beach. In 1962, it was reported that by unanimous vote the city council of Long Beach banned the sport, the only beach in Nassau County where it had been permitted. *Newsday* reported that Long Beach police chief Raymond Panza said the ordinance was passed because "surfboards were a hazard to the bathers" and the city had personal liability suits pending against it.

Up and down the Jersey coast in the early 1960s, there were pockets of surfing activity, largely isolated by inlets, that were unbeknownst to the next pocket of activity even ten miles up or down the coast. These isolated areas banded together when local political battles started drawing surfers together and also after the contest scene started getting off the ground.

By the early to mid-1960s, there were three primary centers of surfing in New Jersey: Long Branch, Belmar and Ocean City. Asbury Park, Seaside Heights and Mannasquan had ordinances on the books banning surfing, some dating as far back as 1952, citing that the beaches were simply too crowded to allow such a sport. "Asbury Park caters to many people rather than just a few," a city employee was reported to say.

Cecil Lear, along with others, set out to change the ordinances by founding the Jersey Surfers, later changed to the Jersey Surfing Association (JSA) in 1963 to avoid confusion with surf fishermen. Lear was the group's president.

By July 1964, the JSA had secured surfing a beach between 5th and 8th Avenues for surfers, with lifeguard protection. The JSA also fielded a six-man patrol to aid lifeguards and help novice surfers. Other protected surfing areas were Long Branch, Seaside Park, Lavallette and Island Beach State Park.

A couple other conflicts were also happening that ultimately helped lead to the founding of the Eastern Surfing Association (ESA). In Florida, the Town of Palm Beach had a very restrictive anti-surfing ordinance. On Dolphin Road lived a town commissioner. Surfing already had a bad reputation, with kids changing clothes in the street, parking their cars on people's lawns and the like. People wanted to ban surfing, and similar anti-surfing ordinances were becoming prevalent up and down the Florida coast. You couldn't even have a surfboard in your possession on Singer Island at Palm Beach Shores.

The local surfers decided that something had to be done. With support from David Aaron and David Reese, a surfer volunteered to get arrested in order to challenge the law in court. The surfer was found guilty, but after appeals, the case went to the Florida Supreme Court, where the surfer won in a ruling that said that surfing could be controlled in the community, but it could not be banned.

The ruling had an immediate impact over the whole state of Florida. Every community had to go along with it. There were a lot of small communities with retired people who fought surfing, so the ruling was significant.

On a larger scale, state Supreme Court rulings could have bearing in other states, since one could take a Florida ruling into a New Jersey or Virginia court as precedent on the state level. The ruling finally came about in 1967 and would ultimately get Reese involved in what would become the ESA.

USSA JUDGES COME EAST

With a growing Grand Prix contest circuit that lured surfers from Maine to Florida, Cecil Lear from Belmar, New Jersey, in conjunction with Webb Brown from Virginia Beach, flew Hoppy Swarts and others from the United States Surfing Association (USSA) out to the Seaside Heights contest in 1967. Their arrival to help judge the contests, along with the cross-pollination of organizers and surfers from other states, soon further set the stage for the founding of the Eastern Surfing Association.

Hoppy Swarts was one of the founders and competition director of the USSA and had organized and judged contests for years on the West

The United States Surfing Association was the umbrella organization that included the Eastern Surfing Association, the Western Surfing Association and the Hawaii Surfing Association. *Courtesy of Pete Smith.*

Coast. As a kid, he came in fifth at the Corona Del Mar Surfing contest in 1928 that Blake won going away and in 1934 won a tandem surfing championship. He graduated from Redondo Beach High School in 1935 and earned a master's degree in electrical engineering from Berkeley. In 1961, he helped found the United States Surfing Association to be the governing body of the sport and focused on organizing and judging competitions along the California coast.

Cecil Lear had joined the USSA in 1965 and corresponded with Swarts for two years as president of the Jersey Surfing Association. Swarts let Lear know he would be in Virginia Beach for the East Coast Surfing Championships.

By this time, Lear had spent the last few years helping to organize and judge contests from Montauk, New York, to Cape May, New Jersey, as well as working to open surfing beaches all over New Jersey. By 1967, there were four hundred members in the Jersey Surfing Association.

At the same time, Rudy Huber of Westport, Connecticut, was president of a group called the SURFari Club International, Ltd., which put together surf trips offering club discounts and other benefits. Huber met the chairman of the International Surfing Federation (ISF), Eduardo Arena, in Lima, Peru, where they discussed the benefits of a network of surfing organizations under the umbrella of the ISF.

Lear then drafted David Reese from Palm Beach to help with the ESA. Reese contributed with all the equipment and horns and came up with a flag system for when surfers couldn't hear the horns in the water. Prior to his ESA involvement, Reese had also helped out with contests held in Jupiter, Lake Worth Pier and Fort Pierce. David Aaron ran the district, and Reese was the competition director.

In the summer of 1967, Cecil Lear got in touch with Webb Brown to suggest that he would be willing to share the costs to bring Swarts, Les Williams and Marge Calhoun out to judge the Atlantic States Contest at Seaside Heights on their way to the East Coast Surfing Championships in Virginia Beach.

Swarts was impressed with the organization of the contests and caliber of surfing. Then one night when Hobie Alter was having dinner with Cecil Lear, Hobie remarked, "Hoppy tells me that you know how to throw a contest. Hoppy thinks you should be a point man and get in touch with Rudy Huber." Soon after, Swarts approached Lear and Huber about establishing the Eastern Surfing Association.

In October 1967, a contest was held in Puerto Rico to commence the establishment of the new organization under the SURFari Club International. At the same time, Huber was working with Arena to bring the world contest in 1968 to Puerto Rico.

The contest was called the SURFari Club International–East Coast Surfing Association and was run in cooperation with the Puerto Rico Department of Tourism and sponsored by Bonne Bell Cosmetics. It was held at Punta Higuaro on the northwest coast. The top surfers from each of seven districts received transportation and lodging. Claude Codgen took first in the men's event, followed by Sam Gornto, Gary Propper, Bruce Clelland and Mike Tabeling.

THE ESA IS ESTABLISHED

The next month, November 1967, Lear met Huber in Westport, Connecticut, to write the constitution and bylaws for the fledgling Eastern Surfing Association, with much guidance from Swarts and Williams, and based largely on the USSA bylaws. At the same time, they got together with Bette Marsh of Atlantic Beach, North Carolina, who organized the very first ESA contest on Memorial Day weekend in 1968.

Huber became the executive director, and Cecil was appointed competition director. Jance Domorski was treasurer. Lear tirelessly traveled up and down the East Coast, organizing at first four large districts and then seven districts from Maine to Florida and the Gulf Coast in what became the largest surfing organization in the world.

The first district directors were Will Jacobs in New England, Don Herd in New York, Richard Duffin in New Jersey, Bob Holland in Virginia Beach, Bette Marsh from North Carolina to Georgia and David Reese in Florida.

In 1968, the Eastern Surfing Association was formally incorporated in Belmar, New Jersey. Swarts had been wanting to decentralize the USSA to make it more responsive on a regional level. Thus, the USSA was abolished, and in addition to the ESA, the Western Surfing Association (WSA) and the

Hawaiian Surfing Association (HSA) were formed as arms of the new United States Surfing Federation (USSF). In addition, Gulf Surfing Association (GSA) was established.

The Grand Prix series sponsored by Dick Van Winkle and *Surfing East* magazine dissolved. A mission statement was announced shortly after ESA's creation. "The primary function of the program is to for the first time, ensure uniformity in both rules and judging in ESA-sanctioned contests," the July 1968 *Surfing News* reported. "It is also hoped that the program will further the understanding of the sport by the non-surfing public and encourage their support in future projects and to improve the existing surfing facilities and to gain new ones."

RULES ARE HONED AND REFINED

At the time, rules and standards of judging tended to vary by beach town. The rules in particular would be honed and refined, including interference and wave possession guidelines, to be strictly enforced. The categories were men's (eighteen to twenty-four), juniors' (fifteen to seventeen), boys' (fourteen and under) and women's (open). Class 1A and 2A competed within these categories, and the winners of each division of Class 2A made it to 3A and then 4A.

"In addition, the experience gained by those involved in this completion program can be utilized to assist high schools and possible colleges in starting surfing competition at the intramural and interscholastic levels," according to *Surfing News*.

An advertising campaign ensued in the major surf magazines, soliciting members through endorsements by Gary Propper, Sam Gornto and Mimi Munro.

The first ESA contest was held on Memorial Day weekend, May 24, 1968, at Wrightsville Beach, North Carolina, under the leadership of Bette Marsh and the local Jaycees. In the 4A men's division, Larry Minniard came in first, followed by Gary Propper, Joe Roland, Vince Roland and Fred Grosskreutz of Virginia Beach. In the men's 3A, it was Warren Bolster, Chuck Kuhn and Mike Bowe. Janice Domorski won the women's division.

Meanwhile, that first ESA contest caused some trauma to the town. A couple of prominent West Coast surfers got arrested for skipping out on their meal tab. It soured the town fathers on surfing, and it was some time before there was another contest in Wrightsville Beach. Mike Angelo, the

ESA attorney, subsequently intervened against the efforts to ban surfing, and partly through the efforts of the ESA, they secured a surfing beach at Mallard Street.

The ESA was divided into seven districts, with each district holding six contests a year and finalists advancing to the championships at Cape Hatteras. In Florida, the contests were held year-round in Fort Pierce, Jacksonville Beach or St. Augustine, New Smyrna Beach, Cocoa Beach and Melbourne Beach to determine who would go to the championships. In Florida, the Easter contest at Canaveral Pier was always the first big contest of the year.

The East Coast competition surf tour took shape—beginning on Memorial Day weekend at Wrightsville Beach; then up to Newport, Rhode Island; winding back down to Gilgo Beach and on to Seaside Heights; then to the East Coast Surfing Championships in Virginia Beach; and finally down to Cocoa Beach for Labor Day. The contests that first year in 1968 featured "unremarkable surf" at Virginia Beach, where Corky Carroll beat Joe Roland in the men's 4A. Bob Holland of Virginia Beach won the senior men's title over George Gerlach of New Jersey and John Hannon of New York.

THE ESA AIMS FOR THE WORLD CHAMPIONSHIPS

The first year of the ESA's contest circuit proved to be a success even though the waves were not particularly good. *Surfing* magazine reported the contests were well organized, with heat sheets posted, along with times and results. The ESA crowned a champion and sent a team to the U.S. and World Championships. The judging, which was always a struggle under the previous Grand Prix format, was seen as more consistent, even if everyone didn't always agree.

In 1969, the ESA, now based out of New York, ran an ad celebrating its first birthday and promising a "new, exciting program" for the coming year, which would culminate at the World Championships in South Africa.

The contest circuit would again stretch the coastline, and while the locals in each town entered, the Floridians traded wins throughout the circuit until returning home for Labor Day.

With the extensive travel and expense involved, and especially considering the erratic quality of the surf, Cecil Lear and the competition committee of the ESA planned in the future to have the contest broken down into specified regions, with a set number of contests in each individual area. The schedule would culminate in a championship contest off the Outer Banks of North Carolina, the East Coast's best surf spot, which just happened to be in a central location and a worthy journey for everyone. By December 1969, *Surfing* magazine was reporting a vote would take place at the next meeting, and hopefully the new plan would be enacted for 1970. However, through this transition, there would be no surfing championships that year. The first ESA Championships would take place at the lighthouse in Buxton in 1971.

Chapter 4

The 1970s and 1980s

From Soul Surfer to Rip and Slash

As the 1970s arrived, America's fascination with surfing waned. Surfing settled into a more countercultural era, more introspective and certainly hedonistic. Now, "expression sessions" were favored by many over competition, which went out of vogue. Surfers embodied an alternative lifestyle and continued the hippie vibe. It was the era of the soul surfer.

The East Coast Surfing Championships faced new challenges as a result. As the luster of surfing dimmed, it was determined that ECSC seemed to intrude rather than enhance the beach experience. Ultimately, the City of Virginia Beach forced a move away from the resort area over to Camp Pendleton, a military base.

A new slew of surf shops sprang up along the coast, some taking the places of venerable 1960s shops that went under with the passing of the surf fad and longboards to the arrival of the shortboards. But with the new shops came new attitude. The surf shop took on the feel of a hippie outpost. Surfers were the counterculture.

Meanwhile, two camps were about to converge on the Outer Banks, one from Virginia and the other from Florida. Bill Frierson, Marty Keesecker, Mike Doyle, Ronnie Mellott, Lynn Shell, Steve Hess and Murray Ross from Virginia; and Ted James, Pete Dooley, Scott Busbey, Greg Loehr and Jim Vaughn from Florida were all at various moments on the Outer Banks, where they experimented with surfboard design, opened shops and manufactured a variety of surfboards all through the 1970s' evolution through shortboards, kneeboards, twin fins, thrusters and more.

By 1972, the Cape Hatteras Lighthouse, iconic and majestic as ever, faced creeping beach erosion, buttressed by sandbags. The dunes finally disappeared, and it became a flat beach. In 1999, the decision was made to move the lighthouse to its present location. *Photo by Ray Couch, courtesy of the Outer Banks History Center.*

In 1970, Lee and Harriet Jones opened up 17th Street Surf Shop. In 1972, on the tenth anniversary of the ECSC, Bob Holland won another (of his total seven) U.S. Championships and was selected as a judge at the 1972 World Surfing Championships in San Diego. A couple years later, Wave Riding Vehicles found new owners in Les Shaw and Bill Frierson.

As surfing evolved along the East Coast, a new group carried on the sport with the rise of New Yorker Ricky Rasmussen, winner of the epic 1974 U.S. Championships in Cape Hatteras, and Floridian Jeff Crawford, who took second at the Easterns in 1971 but shocked the surfing world in 1974 by winning the Pipeline Masters. Likewise, the arrival of the world professional tour to New Jersey and Florida, and the "music revolution" in the late 1970s, reinvigorated and redefined surfing style and heightened the East Coast's visibility in the larger surfing world. Wes Laine of Virginia Beach would establish himself as a world tour professional surfer.

Then came the 1980s, with the "slash, rip and shred" decade of Dayglo wetsuits, New Wave and progressive music and a booming surf clothing industry. Surfing became mainstream again. Surf culture and competition were hot. Major department stores started carrying major surf brands like Quiksilver. Many felt this competition negatively impacted the surf shop industry, since it undercut a key sales ingredient for surf shop businesses—clothing.

In Virginia Beach, Allen White and Gurney Collins each established surfboard manufacturing operations. In the water, Jon Kleintop, Pete Smith Jr., Allen White, Jason Borte and Seth Broudy were top competitors and ECSC surfing champions.

FLORIDIANS SET UP SHOP IN CAPE HATTERAS

In May 1971, in the old post office building and general store in Waves, Barton Decker opened up Hatteras Island Surf Shop. At first, he was open summers only and he sold mostly WRV boards and was one of their first dealers. But he did carry other boards as well.

Meanwhile, Ted James from South Florida had been involved in the surfboard building business since 1968 and was a part of Ocean Avenue Surf Shop. In 1970, he represented the United States in the World Championships in Australia. In May 1974, James moved up from South Florida to Buxton and opened Fox Watersports, just for the summer, which he did the next

The abandoned post office and general store building in Waves was transformed in 1971 into Hatteras Island Surf Shop. *Aycock Brown Collection, courtesy of the Outer Banks History Center.*

year as well. In 1976, he opened up year-round. Jorge Machuca, the Puerto Rican surf champion, came with James. Don Bowers worked as a glasser at Fox for a while. Ted James was a fisherman, first and foremost, but as the windsurfing industry took off and Hatteras became a destination for that sport as well, Fox Watersports diversified its product offerings without the focus on just surfing.

There was also a new group of Florida guys who would find their way to Cape Hatteras as quickly as they could, including Greg Loehr, Pete Dooley and Scott Busbey. Busbey and Loehr went to Cocoa Beach High School together. Dooley was about three years older, and Dooley and Busbey were anxious to build surfboards.

Dooley started shaping in 1968 while living in a 16th Street apartment in Cocoa Beach. He had a lean-to where he made boards. Five blocks down, Greg Loehr was riding for Hobie, Keith Gardner was riding for Weber and Jim Cartland was riding for Catri. Jeff Crawford and Scott Busbey started making shortboards. At the time, both Crawford and Loehr were all over the

99

Left: Barton Decker, founder of Hatteras Island Surf Shop. *Photo by Drew Wilson, courtesy of the Outer Banks History Center.*

Below: Ted James of Fox Watersports in Buxton in the shaping room. James was a surfer and fisherman whose business shifted to windsurfing. *Photo by Drew Wilson, courtesy of the Outer Banks History Center.*

magazines. Along with Ricky Rasmussen, they went to Hawaii and showed they could fit in, these East Coasters, one from New York.

Greg Loehr first came up to Cape Hatteras in 1973 and stayed for four months. While there, he met Lynn Shell, who had just graduated from high school in Virginia Beach and had moved to Buxton. Loehr worked on a garbage truck with Robbie Johnson in the mornings and then surfed all day. When he got back to Florida, Loehr suggested to George Easley and Pete Dooley that they move to Hatteras and build surfboards.

George Easley was riding for Castor Surfboards at the time but wanted to make his own boards. So Easley and Dooley started a line of boards and named it Natural Art. Dooley, Loehr and Busbey built the boards, and Easley helped sell them along the East Coast.

Dooley went on the road to explore the coast, traveling through South and North Carolina. After going to Hatteras, he decided he wanted to relocate there. In 1975, Dooley, Loehr and Busbey set up a manufacturing operation in an old ice factory in Hatteras Village. Business was tight and bare bones, but they were sending boards all over the East Coast. They toughed it out but came back to Florida the same year.

At first they sold 70 boards; after moving back to Florida, they sold 140 boards, then 450. It helped that Greg Loehr won the ESA championships in Hatteras in 1974. Over time, they started selling upward of 2,000 boards. Not only that, but Dooley, Loehr and the crew were now these "mystical guys" who had moved to Hatteras. Now you had the East Coast champ Greg Loehr shaping Natural Art's boards and going to Hawaii, adding even more credibility.

At Hatteras, a core group of surfers challenged any surf that came in. Hurricane Amy in 1975 was memorable. Greg Loehr, Lynn Shell and Scott Busbey were there tearing it up. In 1976, they moved the business back to Florida, where they set up a new factory on Merritt Island. But Busbey, a glasser, wanted to move back to Hatteras. That summer of 1976, Busbey worked for Dooley and then went to Hawaii.

In January 1977, Scott and his wife, Carol Busbey, also an accomplished surfer, returned to Hatteras and in February they opened Natural Art Surf Shop in an old BP gas station. They had a dozen leashes, a half dozen surfboards and a case of wax. In 1978, Lynn Shell started shaping boards for Natural Art and worked at the shop.

The 1970s surf scene in Hatteras was laidback, with a certain underground, intimate quality. You could always expect a thumbs up or down to give you the surf report as you drove down. Many surfers came for weeks or months

In January 1977, Scott and Carol Busbey opened Natural Art Surf Shop in an old gas station. They had a dozen leashes, a half dozen surfboards and a case of wax. *Courtesy of Gary Crawford.*

Lynn Shell at the Kitty Hawk Pier. *Photo by Mickey McCarthy, courtesy of Lynn Shell.*

In 1980, Natural Art Surf Shop moved to its current location. *Courtesy of Lynn Shell.*

at a time, but they also came on weekends, from Friday until Sunday or, if the surf was good, until Monday. By the 1980s, though, many of the Virginia Beach–area surfers would just go to Hatteras for the day, come home, get up and go back the next day.

The Cape Point Campground, Frisco and Frisco Woods were often filled in the 1970s and '80s, with campers from Maine to Florida and beyond to rough it and surf it. Camping at the National Park Service campgrounds was a rite of passage for many surfers from all over the East Coast. It would be a routine of four-a-day surf sessions.

In 1979, after Dooley wanted to take the Natural Art Surfboard brand back to Florida, Scott Busbey began a new board series and called it In the Eye, inspired by Hurricane David. This time, Busbey was the shaper. Busbey started shaping at George Easley's place in Hatteras Village, and Lynn Shell did the finish work. In 1980, Natural Art Surf Shop moved into its location on Highway 12. Shell and Rob Finchem, a friend and local carpenter, helped build it, and Shell was the first employee starting in 1978.

NAGS HEAD/OBX IN THE 1970S

Murray Ross taught school in Northern Virginia and spent summers and holidays on the Outer Banks beginning in 1969. By 1971, he was doing ding repair, and the next year, he started shaping. Cavalier Surf Shop on the beach road continued to have its presence, alternating between functions as a laundromat and a place renting boards and wax.

There was also the ever-present contingent coming down from Virginia Beach to catch the swell and, in many cases, making a permanent move, including Jimbo Ward, Bob Sykes, Steve Thomas (from Northern Virginia), Kevin Payne, Jimbo Brothers, Skip Jones, Skip Saunders and Monty Leavell.

Ben Ward was a lifeguard in Virginia Beach and got a popout board called a Dextra. His brother Jimbo tried it out and, in 1963, when he turned thirteen, got his own board, a Harbour Banana model that he ordered from California. Around this time, Princess Anne County was absorbed into the new City of Virginia Beach. The Wards lived in Kempsville, and Jimbo graduated from Princess Anne High School and later Virginia Wesleyan. With family ties in Currituck County, he took every chance he could to get to the Outer Banks.

There was a place near the Nags Head Pier called the Pink Flamingo, which had been damaged by fire. They got the building cleaned up so it would pass inspection, and that's where Al Sneblin opened Al's Surf Shop around 1966. It was only open for that season. In 1971, Harris Pulley opened a new Harris Surf and Ski in Kill Devil Hills, with Jimbo Ward as the manager. Then, around 1973, Bob DeGabrielle and Jimbo Ward opened a shop called Happiness Boutique and Surf Shop.

Lynn Shell spent much of his early years in Sandbridge during the mid-1960s riding the pumped-up Converse floats and later lifeguarding. From Knott's Island, they would take a boat over to Carova to surf. Some of the Sandbridge guys he surfed with—all older guys—were Gene Snow, Billie Latrelle and his brothers Wesley and Tommy Shell. For a time, Lynn attended Lake Taylor High School in Norfolk, where he was a member of the Surf Club along with Bill and Bob Van, Bill Bartee and some others. Local surf shops WRV and America Surfboards set up displays at club meetings.

After graduating from Bayside High School in 1973, Shell immediately moved to Buxton, working odd jobs and surfing as much as possible. He worked hard to learn any aspect of the surfboard business and at surfing. In 1975, Shell began riding for WRV and made his first trip to the North

Shore in the winter of 1975–76. It was a couple years later that Shell started working at Natural Art in the store while also building surfboards.

Meanwhile, Jim Vaughn was a surfer from Jupiter, Florida. He went away to college at The Citadel in Charleston, where he surfed at Folly Beach. In 1967, he started making trips to the Outer Banks. After graduation, he landed a good job, but he really wanted to own a surf shop. His former roommate Skip Ledingham had a surf shop in Florida called Resin Craft. After a trip to Nags Head, Ledingham agreed to open a second location on the Outer Banks.

They opened as Resin Craft in 1975, with Vaughn as the shop manager. Eventually, Vaughn became a partner and then the owner. In 1977, Vaughn changed the name to Whalebone Junction. Its pirate logo was a bit foreboding as one drove up to Cape Hatteras National Seashore. Along with OP and Sundek and Birdwell Beach Britches, he sold Aipa and Takayama and Channin Surfboards and Surfboards by Don.

Don Bennett remained a surfing force along the Outer Banks who took Vaughn on surfing trips in the classic surfer style: closing shop when the swell was up and heading for the surf. One of Don's team riders and best friends was Joe Marchione, whom Vaughn remembered as the "ultimate underground surfer," which was the style at the time.

The Whalebone pirate logo was a bit foreboding as one headed onto Cape Hatteras National Seashore. *Courtesy of Jim Vaughn.*

Also on Don's team was David "Crockett" Farrow. Inspired by Bruce Sheppard, who was one of the first locals to travel far distances in search of waves, Crockett was off to Hawaii as soon as he turned eighteen, and for the next several years he traveled all around the world in search of waves with friends, including Joe Marchione, Charlie Brown and others. They spent months in Hawaii and then traveled to Bali and Fiji. He and Marchione spent six months in Australia. Marchione himself spent years living in Hawaii. During his travels, Crockett met surfers from Virginia Beach, including Richard "Rail" McGee, Lewis "Twigg" Rogers, Frank "Spot" Russell, Donnie Lassiter and Wendy Mason.

When they came home, they carried the air of surfers who'd been to exotic places and had the stories to back them up. Mostly they could back it up in the local surf, and during the '70s era, they owned the aura of underground surfers. In fact, Crockett had seen a column in *Surfer* magazine called "Soul on Glass," and he put that moniker on many of the boards he owned.

Joe Marchione was born in Norfolk and grew up in Virginia Beach. He won the junior men's division at the ECSC in 1971. After high school, he headed to the Outer Banks but also spent time in Cocoa Beach before moving to Hawaii. Along with Crockett, he established a reputation as one of the best surfers in the area and certainly one of the most hardcore.

For the surfers coming to town from out of the immediate area, Vaughn at Whalebone developed a bit of an "underground" surf report back before shops had toll-free call-in numbers and websites, and certainly before Surfline. Just through word of mouth, surfers from out of the area—including those from Virginia Beach but also from Richmond and elsewhere—developed a system. Back then you could call someone collect, meaning the receiving end would pay for the call, *unless* you didn't get through to the person you were looking to speak to; then there was no charge. The code was to call in to Whalebone and ask for "Murph the Surf," and if the waves were decent, the reply would be that Murph wasn't there but would be back between two and three, as in "two- to three-foot waves." If there was no surf, the reply would be, "He's not here and we don't know when he'll be back."

New to the area, Vaughn started surfing at Jennette's Pier but noticed when no one else was there. That's because Jennette's Pier didn't like surfers, and fishermen were known to cast their sinkers at nearby surfers. If you got caught surfing too close to the pier, the police would confiscate your board, which happened on more than one occasion. The other thing was that there were sharks being caught right from the pier—sometimes really big sharks!

Last chance to get some wax before heading to Cape Hatteras. *Courtesy of Jim Vaughn.*

In 1974, Crockett got bit by a three- to four-foot shark on the south side of Jennette's Pier that put him in the hospital for over two weeks and kept him out of the water for several months.

From 1975 to 1986, no surfing was allowed between 10:00 a.m. and 4:00 p.m. The rule caused an uproar because it also included rent-a-floats and boogie boards. Surfing too close to the pier might get your board confiscated, as happened to Crockett, Sheppard and others.

The boogie board thing put it over the edge, when they too were outlawed. No "hollow or solid floating object" could be used during those hours. Kids couldn't use these during the day in front of their own houses. Jim Vaughn fought this law for eleven years, though some of the town elders may have thought it was just because he wanted to sell more boogie boards.

Joe Domitrouits from Norfolk catches the wave. *Photo by Drew Wilson, courtesy of the Outer Banks History Center.*

On the town council at that time was Larry Gray, an owner of Gray's department store and one of the early Nags Head surfers, along with Gary Oliver, who owned the Outer Banks Pier. Gray and Oliver were both instrumental in having the law changed so that it was okay to use boogie boards so long as you had a leash.

VIRGINIA BEACH SHOPS, SHAPERS AND STICKS

By the early 1970s, Bob White had moved on from WRV to other projects, shaping Man Medium Wave, the Real McCoy and other surfboards before eventually moving to Hawaii. Pete Smith's Surf Shop in 1976 remained at 28th and Pacific under new owner Chuck Conklin. A number of new surf shops opened, not just at the oceanfront but throughout the Tidewater area. Harry Purkey ran Virginia Beach Surf Shop. Around 1974, David Bear, a Norfolk firefighter and district director of the ESA, opened Bear's Surf Shop.

Bill Frierson, meanwhile, had met Les Shaw in the winter of 1969 and then moved to Kitty Hawk around 1970, opening a board-building operation and shop. He lived there for the next four years. Having learned

After Les Shaw and Bill Frierson took over Wave Riding Vehicles in 1974, they moved the shop to Norfolk Avenue, where it remained until it relocated to 19th and Cypress Avenue. *Courtesy of Rick Romano.*

under Bob White and others, Frierson shaped boards for WRV during this era and also spent winters in Florida working for Sunshine Surfboards. By 1974, the owners behind Wave Riding Vehicles were looking to sell. Frierson and Shaw made an offer, which was accepted. The shop was originally on 21st Street, but they looked for a new location, finding an old sawmill several blocks from the beach on Norfolk Avenue.

WRV stayed true to its heritage as a surfboard builder, with Frierson the head shaper and leading up the manufacturing operation. As boards evolved from single to twin to thrusters, the curling porpoise logo could be seen across Virginia Beach and the Hampton Roads area, up and down the coast and around the world, on surfboards, stickers and T-shirts. Along with Frierson, through the late 1970s and early 1980s, Mike Hamil, Tommy Moore, Marty Keesecker and Mike Doyle were key WRV production shapers. Over the years, WRV utilized the talents of a venerable group of surfboard shapers and builders, some of whom moved on to establish their own brands, including Lynn Shell, Allen White, Mike Hamil, Mickey McCarthy, Mike Beveridge and a host of others.

In 1975, Allen White and Marc Bischoff started Offshore Days Surfboard Company. At first, they sold boards to Pete Smith's Surf Shop under new

Allen White started Seasoned Surfboards and then opened Sea Level Surf Shop. *Author's collection.*

owner Chuck Conklin, and then when David Bear opened his shop, he contracted to build the Bearcraft Surfboard label for Bear's Surf Shop.

In 1977, after Bischoff moved off to school, White went to work at WRV for a while and then soon after established his own surfboard line. After throwing around suggestions for a name on a cross-country trip to the U.S. Surfing Championships in San Diego, Carol Busbey suggested Seasoned Surfboards—and that's what stuck. Around this time, White moved to Cocoa Beach and lived there for several years.

In the late 1970s, Mickey McCarthy and Mike Hamil started building boards in Buxton, next to a trailer McCarthy was living in. They called them Sun Surfboards. In 1980, McCarthy and Hamil purchased the building across from the Nags Head Pier where Surfboards by Don was located. But when offered an opportunity, McCarthy moved to Virginia Beach to work for WRV, where Hamil was also a longtime shaper. When McCarthy and his wife, Betsy, moved back to Nags Head, they reopened the shop as New Sun Surfboards.

In 1978, Duncan Currie and Lisa Noonan opened up Vitamin Sea Surf Shop, selling Castor Surfboards and Sunset Surfboards into the 1980s. In Norfolk in 1978, Michael Dolsey opened his company Dolsey Ltd., which began as a company doing industrial work but evolved to a company designing, selling and distributing surfboards and SUVs from a warehouse near Colley Avenue, not just locally but along the East Coast.

Every August, when it was time for ECSC, the Virginia Beach surfers made the most of their home court advantage. In 1970, John Holland won the junior men's division. The next year, in 1971, his father, Bob Holland, won his fourth senior men's East Coast title, while Bob's daughter Honey Holland won the girls' division. Dennis Doyle won the men's title that year.

Bennett Strickland won boys' in 1970 and then lost to Bobby Gardner in 1971. George Desgain won the Jaycee contest.

Jimbo Brothers, already a two-time former ECSC champ, won the 1972 ECSC Pro event over Richard Munson and Gary Propper, while Don Bennett won the senior men's. In the boys' division in 1972, future Virginia Beach shaper Allen White won and then won the junior men's in 1973.

In 1974, Pat McQuilkin won the senior men's, Bennett Strickland won the junior men's, Wes Laine was the boys' champ and Honey Holland won the women's, her second title. In 1975, Marty Keesecker won the masters' division, Allen White the junior division and David Nuckles the boys' division, followed by Wes Laine in second. Honey Holland won her third title in 1976 in women's, and David Nuckles from Myrtle Beach won junior men's. Ben Lane from Virginia Beach won the senior men's in 1973, 1977 and 1978.

Wes Laine won the junior men's in 1978; David Nuckles won the men's. Marty Keesecker won the longboard and senior men's events in 1978 and 1979. Allen White won the men's in 1979.

THE EASTERN SURFING ASSOCIATION

By the early 1970s, Cecil Lear had bowed out of a formal role in the ESA as competition director. Huber continued as executive director until around 1970. Doc Couture became district director in New England in 1969. David Reese continued to run the Florida district until 1972, and Bette Marsh anchored the Southeast. In the very beginning, the mid-Atlantic was a large district that extended from Ocean City, Maryland, to Atlantic Beach, North Carolina.

In 1970, Virginia Beach and the Outer Banks split off and became its own district. David Bear, who owned Bear's Surf Shop, covered the Virginia Beach/Outer Banks district. Then in 1980, Ben Lane petitioned that the Virginia/Outer Banks District be split into two districts. In November 1980, Dorothy Dunn became director of the new Outer Banks district after it split off from Virginia Beach. It seems the Outer Banks guys didn't like going to Virginia Beach as much as the Virginia Beach guys liked going to the Outer Banks.

On the competitive side, Dunn was herself a champion surfer who in 1982 won her division at the U.S. Championships held in Buxton. The ESA moved to a regional championships format in 1985 leading up to the ESA Championships.

Above: Surfers and spectators gather on the Outer Banks during a contest. It's mostly surfboards with single fins, but notice there's also a twin fin on the beach. *Aycock Brown Collection, courtesy of Outer Banks History Museum.*

Left: Yancey Spencer, Jimbo Brothers and Fletcher Christian on the beach at ECSC in 1971. *Courtesy of Yancey Spencer.*

In 1972, David Reese, district director covering St. Augustine to Miami, became competition director for the ESA Championships in Hatteras, which he ran until 1978. Bette Marsh, meanwhile, took on the biggest geographical territory, covering southern North Carolina to Georgia. David Bear became the ESA district director covering Virginia Beach and the Outer Banks. It was a strong district, with Greg Loehr, Randy Laine and Wes Laine part of it.

In 1971, the ESA sent its top six surfers to the U.S. Championships in Huntington Beach, with three placing in the finals, the highest in second. In all, forty-five members from the ESA traveled to the contest, of whom twenty-seven entered.

At the same time, the ESA was beginning to suffer the fallout of society's new indifference to surfing, and membership began to lag. To raise funds, Weldon Bankston arranged to have ten surfboards donated by Dyno Manufacturing Company, spread across the ESA districts. He held a raffle, selling tickets for $1.50 each, which helped keep the organization afloat. For his efforts, he was named executive director in 1972. Weldon, originally from Maryland, helped create the man-on-man format and also organized the 1972 Easter contest. He aspired for pro surfing on the East Coast.

Meanwhile, a pro surfing tour was the ambition of many. In the spring of 1972, the ESA, under Bankston, sanctioned the first pro surfing contest on the East Coast at Atlantic Beach, North Carolina. Yancy Spencer from Pensacola (the Gulf Coast) early on distinguished himself as a steady professional surfer. His contest record was outstanding, winning the East Coast Pro in Atlantic Beach in 1972 and the ECSC Pro Division in Virginia Beach in 1973.

Judging standards continued to be a focus in the ESA, which announced a team of thirty certified judges for "a good and fair contest." The ESA added legitimacy to the contests. Until then, contests were run by Jaycee and civic organizations not necessarily focused on uniform judging standards. Judges were usually locals, and no standardized rules existed from contest to contest.

ECSC VERSUS THE ESA CHAMPIONSHIPS

A sign of the decline of surfing's status came when the City of Virginia Beach decided in 1970 to remove the ECSC from the Steel Pier in the resort area. At first, the city sought to move it to Sandbridge/Little Island Park, just about as far away from the resort as you could get. The Virginia

Surfing Association, under the leadership of H. Jack Jennings Jr., opposed the move, not only because the Steel Pier offered the best waves but also because of the isolation of Sandbridge and lack of accommodations at the contest site. Ultimately it was relocated to the National Guard base at Camp Pendleton, a military base. With George Desgain as competition director, the event was considered a success. Virginia governor Linwood Holton and his family attended the event. ECSC remained at Camp Pendleton until the mid-1980s.

During the 1960s, the ECSC was the officially sanctioned event by the USSF crowning the East Coast champion. But the ESA (as part of the USSF) expressed dissatisfaction with the restrictive ordinances of the City of Virginia Beach in moving the contest to Camp Pendleton. It sought to remove its sanction of the event after the 1970 contest.

The ESA wanted to utilize the name "East Coast Surfing Championships," but the Virginia Beach Jaycees fought that. Instead of litigating the matter, ESA changed the name to the Eastern Surfing Championships and staged its first contest in 1971 at Cape Hatteras. At the inaugural 1971 ESA Championships at the Buxton Lighthouse, Charlie Baldwin won over Greg Loehr.

PROFESSIONAL SURFING ON THE EAST COAST

By the early 1970s, the basic trajectory for those who had won all the amateur surfing contests was to try to make money at it. There was controversy, though, with people competing in both amateur and professional events, and lines had yet to be clearly drawn. In order to keep some of these surfers within the umbrella of the ESA, a pro division was developed.

As early as 1971, Weldon Bankston was hoping to make the judges of the ESA 3A/4A contests the backbone for an Eastern Professional Surfing Contest. But controversy erupted within the organization. Not only did Bankston want to go pro with what had been a proudly amateur organization, but he also considered moving the Eastern Surfing Championships to Florida and was amenable to postponing or even canceling a contest if the surfers voted not to run it due to poor conditions, even if conditions were sizable but sloppy.

With a pro surfing tour the ambition of many, in the spring of 1972, the ESA under Bankston sanctioned the first Eastern Professional Surfing Contest, appropriately called the East Coast Pro, at Atlantic Beach, North Carolina. Yancy Spencer from Pensacola won the event and early on distinguished himself as a professional surfer. He also won the ECSC pro division in Virginia Beach in 1973.

But there was still division. The contests were always under pressure because of judging or wave quality or something. Plus, there was a need to separate the amateurs and the pros, without crossover. The majority of the ESA and Bankston were at odds in what direction to pursue regarding a professional ESA circuit, and they went their separate ways.

Colin "Doc" Couture was given the nod as the new executive director. He quickly got things organized, was very diplomatic and got charters and paperwork done. At the time, there were about one thousand members in the ESA.

THE ESA'S HATTERAS HOME

David Reese from Palm Beach became competition director in 1972, responsible solely for the annual contests at Hatteras. He wrote and helped formalize judging rules, such as who had possession of the wave and when. Also volunteering and helping to judge were Linda Hanson from New York and Ruth Grottola from New Jersey.

At the ESA Championships in 1973, Mike Oppenheimer of New York challenged Greg Loehr in the finals of the men's division. Greg "selected the rights while Mike worked the lefts" in Tropical Storm Christine's surf, with a unanimous decision for Oppenheimer. In the junior men's division, it was Ricky Rasmussen of New York, while Skill Johnson of Ocean City, Maryland, won the senior men's, Toni Bryant was the women's champ and Dick Catri won the masters'. The winners got trips to California.

With the surfing boom waning from its heyday in the '60s, and with a growing anti-competitive spirit, Couture expanded the nature and scope of the organization while still continuing the competitive circuit. Now, the ESA offered scholarships, embraced environmental issues and dealt with beach access.

While the late 1960s had featured more of a Grand Prix format, with travel to events in the very large districts, beginning in the early 1970s, districts started dividing out competition in smaller districts to make it more localized and convenient. As a result, membership began to grow.

Couture helped the ESA during the crucial years of a backlash against competition surfing in the 1970s. He created an environment for surfers to develop as competitors. He helped build a tremendous following for the ESA, allowing the districts to grow.

Ultimately, the ESA contest circuit, capped by the annual Eastern Surfing Championships in Buxton, became the training ground for an up-and-coming group that included Jeff Crawford, Greg Loehr and Charlie Baldwin from Florida; Eric Penney, Mike Oppenheimer and Ricky Rasmussen from New York; Dave Sledge, Eric Sledge, Mike Beschen and Mark Neustadter from New Jersey; Skill Johnson, Al Johnson and Terry Sterner from Ocean City, Maryland; Randy Laine, Wes Laine and Allen White from Virginia Beach; Mike Marsh and Mickey Marsh from Atlantic Beach, North Carolina; Will Allison and Bill Curry from Wrightsville Beach; and David Nuckles from Myrtle Beach, South Carolina.

These and other surfers came through the ranks and excelled. From Maine to Florida, surfers cut their competitive teeth throughout the ESA, with the ultimate goal each year of going to the championships at Cape Hatteras.

In 1974, 1978 and again in 1982, the U.S. Championships took place at the lighthouse before moving to Sebastian Inlet in 1986 and then Montauk, New York, in 1990. At the 1978 contest, the Hawaiian team came to Buxton for the first time. The waves were good, and the Hawaiians went away impressed.

Every year, the ESA held the Eastern Surfing Championships—the "Easterns"—in Cape Hatteras, fueled by Doc Couture's belief that Hatteras was the spiritual home of East Coast surfing. To that end, Doc wanted to see to it that the ESA had a permanent presence on the Outer Banks. His plan was to purchase an old hotel, use it as a headquarters for summer surf camps, rent it out to surfers and others the rest of the year and host the annual championships each September. Backed by David Reese, Cecil Lear and Mark Allison, they purchased an old hotel and renamed it the Surf Motel, giving the ESA a year-round presence in Cape Hatteras.

THE ESA AND U.S. CHAMPIONSHIPS ARE HELD IN BUXTON

The year 1974 set a new milestone in East Coast surf history. First, Ricky Rasmussen won the U.S. Championships at Hatteras. Conditions were good in both contests, with sets rolling in chest to overhead, surf that made East Coasters proud to have all those Californians in town to witness it. Then, in December, ESA veteran Jeff Crawford won the Pipeline Masters on the North Shore of Hawaii. That was a huge moment.

The timing for the 1974 Eastern Surfing Championships was perfect, with northeaster surf, and there were real showdowns at the Eastern and again at the U.S. Championships right after. Surf was great for both events. In the contest, Greg Loehr beat Jim Cartland in the men's division as they battled in chest to overhead perfect conditions. By now, Loehr shaped boards for Natural Art and lived on Hatteras Island full time.

The United States Surfing Championships were held immediately following the ESA Championships and represented a coming of age for the East Coast and Cape Hatteras, which was hosting the first ever U.S. Championships held outside California.

David Nuuhiwa, Michael Ho and several Californians and Hawaiians came for the contest. There was great hope that the surf would be good. David Reese ran the contest and consulted with Buddy Hooper about how the weather might impact conditions. Those who knew Hatteras could always predict Hatteras, and Hooper predicted the northeasterly wind would switch. Sure enough, there were three days of northeast swell with southwest winds that produced glassy overhead waves. It was epic, and for many from the outside surfing world, it was the first time they witnessed solid East Coast surf.

Greg Loehr, Tony Staples, Ricky Rasmussen and Jim Cartland battled it out. Under the double-elimination format, they battled one another in rotation. In the finals, Rasmussen faced Cartland from Satellite Beach, Florida. A North versus South matchup, it was a shootout, and "with night falling, several people pulled their jeeps on the beach, shining their headlights to the lineup" reported *Surfer*. It got too dark, so the contest was continued until the next morning. With the surf still good, Rasmussen won it. He also won the kneeboard contest.

Soon after, Rasmussen surprised and impressed the surfing world in Hawaii, riding Pipeline during epic days. He was respected by the international surfers, though something of an oddity being from New York. Born in 1955, Ricky Rasmussen grew up in Westhampton on Long Island, a wealthy beach community. Rasmussen started surfing at age ten, competing in the ESA's New York district. He was able to travel a fair amount and was featured on the ABC network TV show *American Sportsman*. In 1978, he moved to Bali in Indonesia, where it was not unusual to sleep in treehouses. It was reported that he lived with his girlfriend in a treehouse nicknamed "Swiss Family Rasmussen." However, serious trouble was ahead, and after scrabbles with the law and attempts to cooperate, he was shot and killed in Harlem in 1982 in a deal gone bad.

Of course, it was Jeff Crawford—who had finished a tough second at the 1971 ESA contest—who stunned the surfing world in 1974 when he won the Pipeline Masters, the most prestigious surfing contest in the world. In doing so, he took the East Coast to perhaps its highest esteem. Against the likes of Gerry Lopez, Jeff Hayman and Rory Russell, he won the contest. Two years later, in 1976, Crawford finished in the top sixteen on the world tour.

SURF EXPO HATCHED IN VIRGINIA BEACH

In 1975, Ben Lane and David Bear shared leadership of the Virginia/Outer Banks district of the ESA. The U.S. Championships moved to South Padre Island, Texas, in 1975, to Hawaii in 1976 and to Huntington Beach in 1977. In 1978, the U.S. Championships returned to the lighthouse, and this time, the Hawaiian Surfing Association (HSA) brought its team.

In addition, one of the famed Bronzed Aussies, world champion Peter Townend, was also at the contest. Again, the surf came through, and both winners were from the East Coast: Tim Briers and Mary Ann Hayes, both from Florida. In the U.S. Championships that followed at the lighthouse, Californian Tom Curran, soon to be a three-time world champion, won the boys' division. Wes Laine won the junior kneeboard category. Fred Grosskreutz, also from Virginia Beach, won the masters'. In the grand masters' division, Bob Holland won the event over four others from the Western Surfing Association (WSA). Everyone was impressed with the caliber of the surf, which gave not only credibility but also pride to the East Coast surfing scene.

Despite an anti-competitive mentality of the mid-'70s, the human tendency to organize and improve things continued unabated. In 1975, at an ESA board meeting in a Virginia Beach hotel, some industry reps had an impromptu trade show in their hotel rooms, showing their new lines. Ross Houston was the founder of Atlantic Surfing Materials and an ESA beach access director out of Miami Beach. Along with Couture and the rest of the board, they established that a surf convention would be held. In 1976, the first Surf Expo was held in Cocoa Beach in the Cape Colony Hotel, with thirty booths featuring primarily surfboard manufacturers.

By 1978, Surf Expo was being called the largest surf trade show in history and was moved to the Melbourne Civic Auditorium. It was jammed with exhibitors from all over North America and visitors from Japan, Australia, South America and Europe. Among the surfers in attendance were Gerry Lopez, Shaun Tomson and Hobie Alter. By its fifth year, it had 150 booths and was moved to Orlando. It was promoted as a perfect opportunity for shops to see and compare a wide range of products under one roof at one time and was seen as a chance to bring the industry together and encourage cooperation, sponsorships and growth.

Through 1979, the ESA continued to expand under Doc's leadership, and by the mid-1980s, membership had jumped to around four thousand members. Moreover, Doc successfully introduced "official sponsors" to amateur surfing, the first of which was Bill Yerkes's Florida clothing company, Sundek.

In the contentious world of surfing politics, not much had changed, but if anything, it had gotten worse. The surfing image, once fairly clean cut and the envy of a nation, had mirrored the 1970s long-haired, antiestablishment look. Nonetheless, local surfing organizations were still doing good works for beach access and environmental issues. In Virginia Beach, Bill Frierson, Paul West and others led a group of surfers to Richmond in the late 1970s over beach access issues and surfing at Camp Pendleton.

SURFBOARD DESIGN EVOLVES FROM SINGLE FIN TO TWIN FIN TO THRUSTER

When Australian Mark Richards won his first International Professional Surfers (IPS) World Championship riding a twin fin surfboard, people took notice—of the twin fin. The "twin" was shorter and much more maneuverable. World Champion Shaun Thomson, on the other hand, rode the traditional single fin, which fit his down-the-line style in the barrel. Though controversial, twin fins gained acceptance, but there was a divide between those who were committed to single fins and those who liked the twin.

Along came the three-fin thruster that Simon Anderson introduced in 1980. Randy Laine of Virginia Beach, who had been on the IPS tour, knew Anderson when he was coming up with the early three-fin thruster designs. One of them was a six-foot, four-inch square tail thruster. Rusty Preisendorfer, who was shaping for Randy's younger brother Wes, saw it. Soon it was obvious there was something beyond twin fins, and Wes Laine began riding thrusters. By the early 1980s, almost everyone was riding a thruster.

The 1970s became a great time for development and change in surfing attitude from that of an art form to a competitive endeavor that required great conditioning and devotion. The 1970s continued the transition from longboard to shortboard and from single fin to twin fin and finally three fins. From the late 1960s to the early 1980s, surfing evolved from elegantly walking to the nose and hanging ten to the new style of banging off the bottom of the wave, then banging off the top.

THE 1980s USHERS IN NEW SURF CULTURE

Along with surfboard design revolution, there was a music revolution going on that redefined and reenergized the surfing world. In the midst of disco and Led Zeppelin came punk. Now it was the Clash and the Ramones who were energizing the culture, along with groups like the Police and the Cars that had a new "modern" sound. In conjunction with the new high-performance boards, there was a more aggressive style of surfing.

There was a new look as well. Dayglo made a comeback. Wetsuits went from dull scuba black to Dayglo pink, orange and green, and surf trunks oftentimes sported bright, frenzied designs. Gone were the classic, understated baggies with floral print and muted colors. Rip and slash became the new surfing style. The goal became to destroy the waves, shred them, rip them up. A new aggression hit surfing, and the '60s and '70s image of the "soul surfer" gave way to the "Surf Nazi."

A series of new surf magazines started springing up, some aspiring to be the next *Surfer*. These included *Surf* magazine, published by Mike Mann and Alan Margolis. Then were was *Wave Rider/Skate Rider* during the big '70s skateboard boom. Then there was *Swell* magazine. *Shred* magazine, by

Craig Watson rides a wave. *Photo by Drew Wilson, courtesy of the Outer Banks History Center.*

David Neff and John Hutchinson from Virginia Beach, was published in the late 1980s.

During the '80s, surfing's allure came back to the masses. Always on the leading edge of fashion, surf clothing became a hot item, and the surf lifestyle clothing manufacturers were overjoyed with orders. A controversy arose, though, when manufacturers started distributing clothing into chain department stores in direct, and sometimes unfair, competition with what previously had been their bread-and-butter customers, the surf shops. Major department stores bought merchandise in large quantities and at steeper discounts, putting the corner surf shop at a disadvantage. The surf retail industry made its concerns known, and as a result, some surf clothing companies came out with two lines: one for department stores and the other for surf shops.

Nonetheless, many surf shops that started back in the 1970s in shacks and near-condemned buildings selling boards and a few T-shirts were now expanding into gleaming new buildings and suburban malls and selling a diverse line of high-quality "lifestyle" clothing.

THE ESA CHAMPIONSHIPS IN THE 1980S

As the '80s took off with their new prosperity, amateur surfing was the beneficiary as the ESA expanded through new sponsorships. In 1982, the ESA championships were held as usual in Hatteras, but for a change, the U.S. Championships were held at Sebastian Inlet in Florida.

Will Allison of Wrightsville Beach won the men's division in 1980 at the ESA Championships, the first North Carolinian to do so. Also, a hot new group of surfers were coming up: David Spier, Alex Cox and Danny Melhado from Indialantic; Scott Bouchard from Satellite Beach; and Kelly Slater from Cocoa Beach.

In the early 1980s, Dick Catri trained the hot kids every weekend, coaching them on competitive surfing strategies. Sean and Kelly Slater, Todd Holland, Sean O'Hare and others met on Sundays for practice. It was some of the first coaching any of them would get. Bill Yerkes at Sundek sponsored them with trunks, and Matt Kechele started making some of Kelly's early boards.

Slater competed in local contests through the ESA as a kid and competed at the 1983 ECSC in Virginia Beach. At age ten, he won contests against older kids. He was doing aerials and 360s and all the hottest maneuvers.

In 1982, in his second trip to Hatteras for the ESA Championships, he won the Menehune division, and then he won championships each year after that through 1987—six ESA Championships. He also won four U.S. Championships, from 1984 to 1987.

In 1984, the National Park Service did not grant access to the lighthouse for the championships, and the competition was moved to Salvo, north of Buxton. Rich Rudolph won the men's and Bill Johnson the junior men's title. Bill Frierson (of Virginia Beach) took senior men's honors, while Bob Holland won the grand masters' division over George Gerlach. Crystal Roever won the junior women's title, Cheryl Scott the women's and Janice Aragon the senior women's division. Not least, Kelly Slater won the Menehunes division over John Logan and David Speir. Scott Farnsworth and Janice Aragon earned trips to the 1984 World Championships as well. Bob Holland, through his influence, helped to return the contest to the lighthouse in 1985.

In 1986, Kelly Slater won the boys' division at the lighthouse for his sixth ESA Championship. Others began their competitive rise through the mid-1980s. From Virginia Beach came Jason Borte and Seth Broudy, the latter of whom won the 1985 ECSC boys' division, and Pete Smith Jr., who won the juniors' ECSC in 1985. Ocean City, Maryland, produced Chad Hopkins, and New Jersey claimed Dean Randazzo. Likewise, Jay Gould from New Hampshire was strong.

To channel competitive energy and give something back to the sport, Lee Jones of 17th Street Surf Shop in Virginia Beach and Jeff Thomson of Billabong, the clothing manufacturer, sponsored an amateur circuit beginning in 1987 called the Billabong/17th Street Summer Surf Series. Contests took place in Ocean City, Maryland, and on the Outer Banks. Wes Laine was the team coach, and Pete Smith Jr. was among several top competitors on the team.

Meanwhile, the National Scholastic Surfing Association (NSSA) continued to be a significant competitor to the ESA, and through the '80s, its presence along the East Coast solidified. The NSSA was founded in 1978 as a "scholastic" surfing organization, and it did have high school and college teams. It was centered more in Florida and the Southeast, and its annual championship was usually held at Sebastian Inlet. It did compete for surfers with the ESA and got its share, and there was a rivalry between the two.

In the 1989–90 NSSA Florida Conference, Seth Broudy of Virginia Beach was victorious in the men's division, followed by Dean McManus,

In its first year, the Billabong/17th Street contest circuit consisted of four events: two in Virginia Beach; one in Ocean City, Maryland; and one in Cape Hatteras. By 1988, Florida was added to the tour, and later, Rhode Island. By 1989, there were five hundred competitors vying for merchandise and trips to California. *Courtesy of Lee and Harriet Jones.*

John McDaniels and Darron Nettles. Meanwhile, Paul Reinecke won the 1990 ESA and U.S. championships.

On December 14, 1989, Colin "Doc" Couture died. Following Doc's death, the board of the Eastern Surfing Association voted at the Hatteras championships to establish an annual award given in honor of his more than two decades of service. It was the highest award one could achieve with the ESA for outstanding volunteer service.

ECSC IN THE 1980S

There was sometimes a clash of cultures between the guys from Virginia Beach and the Outer Banks. Crammed into a small space at the jetty on 1st Street, often fighting over few-and-far-between swells, the VB guys were maybe a bit more competitive and aggressive when it came to waves. On the Outer Banks, there were plenty of waves to go around, oftentimes good waves, and it was a much smaller community, especially before Memorial Day and after Labor Day. The guys from Wanchese, Manteo, Nags Head,

Kill Devil Hills and Kitty Hawk for the most part all got along, with plenty of goodwill for one another. But sometimes different styles in the water created tension, and seeing Virginia license plates could put some on guard.

As the 1980s rolled in and surfing entered a new boom era, Virginia Beach was part of a much larger metropolitan area with busy year-round surf shops like WRV and 17th Street. While some of the mainstays on the Outer Banks might be more used to surfing in cutoffs, the VB guys would come down in the latest fashions—over the years it ranged from surf trunks to jams and then later boardshorts—and sometimes stood out with their bright colors and frenzied designs,

Competitively, the Virginia Beach surfers remained strong. As the 1980s began, Wes Laine emerged as the major force to be reckoned with, winning the pro division in both 1980 and 1981. In the Menehune division in 1980, another Virginia Beach family prodigy, Pete Smith Jr., won over Jason Binford. Pete Smith Jr. won the junior men's in 1984 and again in 1985. Another big sensation out of Virginia Beach was Jon Kleintop. In 1984, Kleintop won the men's division at ECSC after coming in third the previous year. In the boys' division, Seth Broudy won in both 1984 and 1985. Drew Todd won Menehune in 1985 and boys' in 1987. Drew's brother Chris won Menehune in 1986. In 1988, Jason Borte won the men's title.

Meanwhile, surfers from the 1960s and 1970s started showing up at contests in the 1980s. In 1980, Lynn Shell won the longboard. In 1984, Pete Lively won the masters'. Bill Frierson won senior men's in 1985, beating Will Allison and Jimmy Parnell. In 1987, David Neff won the longboard over Will Allison. In 1986 and 1987, Bobby Holland won senior men's. In 1988, Jon Kleintop won the masters' division. In 1990, in the forty-five and over category, Bob White beat Jett Colanna and George Desgain for the ECSC title. In the thirty-four-to-forty-four group, Bobby Holland beat Jimmy Parnell.

The next generation came up, with Ian Parnell, son of '60s-era Steel Pier sensation Jimmy Parnell, winning the Menehune in 1988 and 1989. (Seven years later, in 1996, Ian would win the men's.) In 1989, Jason Griffith won the boys' and Brad Beach the men's.

On the pro circuit, the ECSC was the oldest contest and annually offered the most prize money. While the first seven contests had been held at the Steel Pier, the next fifteen years the contest was moved to Camp Pendleton. Then in 1985, when the National Guard planned other uses for Camp Pendleton, the city agreed to allow the ECSC to use its original location at 1st through 4th Streets.

Upon its return, the Jaycees broadened the scope of the ECSC, bringing in skateboarding, volleyball, skimboarding, wind surfing and a 5K race. During the mid-1980s, two Floridians dominated the pro ECSC divisions. Rich Rudolph won it in 1985 and 1986, while Scott McCranels of Palm Beach won it back to back in 1987 and 1988.

In Florida, there were contests in Jacksonville, Daytona, New Smyrna Beach and Cocoa Beach, the latter on Labor Day for the annual National Kidney Foundation ASP East Pro/Am, hosted by the Salick brothers and sponsored by Ron Jon. Ron Dimenna gave Ron Jon its start in 1962 in New Jersey, and it became the largest and probably first twenty-four-hour surf shop in the world. Also during the 1980s was a competitive pro surfing contest circuit, with Rich Rudolph, Scott McCranels, Steve Anest and Charlie Kuhn out of Florida dominating. Steve Anest of Ormond Beach won the 1989 ECSC and made it into the ASP World Tour at the turn of the decade.

In 1988, Mike Martin out of New Smyrna Beach started a new pro tour called the APS East. It featured ten events, with most in Florida and a couple in Puerto Rico and Barbados and the granddaddy of them all, the East Coast Surfing Championships in Virginia Beach. Rich Rudolph dominated, winning the first two ASP East titles in 1988 and 1989. On the women's side, Frieda Zamba won the first of her four World Championships in 1984. Zamba, a former ESA competitor from Flagler Beach, won four world titles, from 1984 to 1986 and again in 1988.

VB/OBX IN THE 1980S

By the end of the 1970s, Allen White had won four ECSC titles, plus a top five at the U.S. Championships. In 1983, he and some partners opened Sea Level Surf Shop, located at 24th and Pacific in Virginia Beach. White was living in Florida but traveled the East Coast frequently, for contests and also as a rep for Astrodeck. With the shop just getting underway, Allen moved back to Virginia Beach to help run it. His travels helped him get Seasoned Surfboards into shops on the coast. David Barnes came on board, and in 1985, he was offered a partnership in order to run production in the factory.

Meanwhile, WRV and 17th Street surf shops both showed signs of growth. 17th Street carried Canyon Surfboards out of San Diego and sponsored Wes Laine, the premier surfer not just from Virginia Beach but from the East Coast. When 17th Street Surf Shop was later sold, the Cocke family expanded to ten locations stretching from the Outer Banks to Richmond.

In 1986, WRV moved from its Norfolk Avenue headquarters to a new building on Cypress and 19th Street, the same area where back in the late 1960s Eastside and West Wind Surfboards and Surfboards by Don were built. It also opened a store in Kitty Hawk, managed by Mickey Bednarek, and a shop in Hawaii. With a new WRV location in Kitty Hawk as an anchor, in 1987 WRV moved its surfboard manufacturing operation down as well, to Currituck County.

During this era, Robert "Redman" Manville was an important shaper at WRV. Redman (1952–2004) was from California and manufactured boards on a production basis for Dewey Weber and Donald Takayama, among many others. He moved east to work for WRV and brought some guys to work with him. He gained such a reputation working for WRV, Hatteras Glass and others that *Surfer* magazine credited him as an "East Coast shaping legend."

Other new shapers were coming on board. In 1983, Tim Nolte, from Virginia Beach, started shaping surfboards. In 1984, Gurney Collins started Hotline Surfboards. In 1985, Mike Beveridge, who got his start with New Sun, made Shaped by Beveridge, followed by Surfblades in 1988.

Jesse Fernandez moved up from Florida to the Outer Banks in 1990 to work for WRV with Redman and Tommy Moore. Fernandez did the glass work. Mike Clark, later with Clark Shapes, started shaping in 1998, working with Redman, who he worked with for many years at WRV. In 1991, Bob Yinger moved from California to work at WRV.

Steve Hess from Norfolk opened Secret Spot Surf Shop in Nags Head in 1982. He had been surfing since the 1960s and spent summers in Kitty Hawk back in the 1970s. Hess and Mike Price started making boards called Secret Spot in 1977, and five years later, Hess opened Secret Spot Surf Shop. Hess made his boards where you could watch him work along with Murray Ross, Ted Kearns and Mike Price. Hess also ran the Outer Banks Surf Classic in 1985.

Also in Norfolk, there was a dedicated and hardcore group of surfers and shapers who competed in ECSC and at Hatteras and also traveled the world for surf. These included Scott McCaskey, a surf journalist as well as a competitor; Tim Pope, a Maury alum and dedicated surfer; and Ken Trinder, who also built and shaped boards.

In 1986, with a new planer as a gift from the Busbeys, Lynn Shell moved on from Natural Art. He was now a rep for Town and Country and started creating boards under his own ShellShapes, while also taking jobs doing all aspects of board building, including shaping, polishing, glossing and whatever needed to be done. In 1987, he became a shaper for WRV but also

Bob Crutchfield of Nags Head speeds down the line on a cold winter wave in March 1989. *Photo by Drew Wilson, courtesy of the Outer Banks History Center.*

WRV moved from its Norfolk Avenue building to its current location at 19th and Cypress in 1986. *Author's collection.*

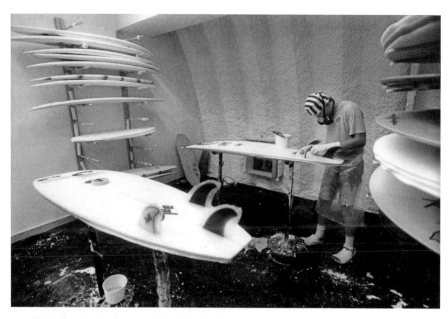

Above: Steve Tabor laminates on fins in 1987 in Harbinger, North Carolina, where the WRV factory was relocated from Virginia Beach. *Photo by Drew Wilson, courtesy of the Outer Banks History Center.*

Left: New Sun shaper Murray Ross lays out a template for a customer, Dan Wilfong, in 1990. *Photo by Drew Wilson, courtesy of the Outer Banks History Center.*

helped out with Allen White and David Barnes at Seasoned Surfboards, Gurney Collins at Hotline and Scott Busbey at Natural Art. Town and Country was one of the major Hawaii surf brands at the time; it later morphed into Hawaiian Island Creations (HIC), under which ShellShapes HIC was a top line.

Meanwhile, after several years shaping for WRV in Virginia Beach, Mickey McCarthy and his wife moved back to the Outer Banks and got New Sun Surfboards up and running.

Rascoe Hunt won his first ESA contest in 1982 and soon after became the first member of the New Sun surf team. In 1987, Murray Ross, Hunt and Steve Head started working at the New Sun factory on the beach road, in the old Surfboards by Don building across from the Nags Head Pier. McCarthy shaped boards, Murray did shaping and sanding and Rascoe did laminating and polishing. Head was also there shaping, and Ted Kearns did sanding and polishing. Mike Rowe also did production work. Mike Beveridge started at New Sun as a polisher and sander and then shaped his first board in 1982. Other good surfers were Eric Dreibelbis and Jordan Ford.

Manufacturing surfboards in a building along the beach road not zoned for use of resins and other materials was a problem, so in 1990, they moved to Ocean Commerce Park. With a burgeoning return to longboard-style surfing, business was good, and there was demand for both longboards and shortboards at beach towns from Maryland to Maine. Shapers would take a line of their boards and usually drive them north up the coast to get them in shops. Florida board builders had bigger reach into the Southeast.

In the old days, a surfboard builder did all aspects of building the board—shaping, glassing, sanding—but the trend in California was that glass work was subbed out to "glass houses." Following that trend, in 1992, Rascoe and Kearns formed Gale Force Glassing (GFG) and did the glassing work for New Sun, Gurney Collins at Hotline and others. Then, Hunt and Kearns started Gale Force Surfboards. Eventually, Rascoe bought out Kearns, who moved on to other things but continued to do some shaping.

Much as WRV brought along a lot of shapers, New Sun did the same for a new generation, many of whom started their own lines. McCarthy brought along a lot of young shapers like Ted Kearns and his TK boards; Mike Rowe, who started Hooked Surfboards; Rascoe Hunt with GFG; and Steve Head and Mike Beveridge with their own boards. At the same time, Mickey

Above: Steve Head near the Nags Head Pier in July 1990. *Photo by Drew Wilson, courtesy of the Outer Banks History Center.*

Right: New Sun shaper Steve Head is seen here wearing the Whalebone Surf Shop team hat in 1990. *Photo by Drew Wilson, courtesy of the Outer Banks History Center.*

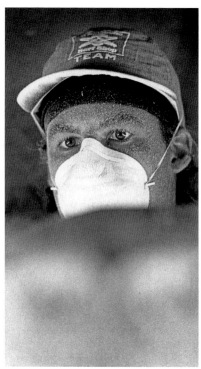

Employees of the Gallery restaurant in Waves, North Carolina, pose with their boards in July 1989. *Photo by Drew Wilson, courtesy of the Outer Banks History Center.*

New Sun glasser Rascoe Hunt of Kill Devil Hills pours resin on the bottom of a board, 1990. *Photo by Drew Wilson, courtesy of the Outer Banks History Center.*

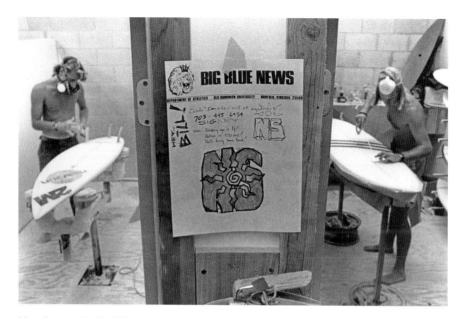

New Sun sander Ted Kearns, *left*, and artist Ben Spruill work at the Ocean Commerce Park surfboard manufacturing facility in August 1990. *Photo by Drew Wilson, courtesy of the Outer Banks History Center.*

started being recognized for his work as a surf photographer. His images were published in *Eastern Surf Magazine*, *Surfer* and others. After a while, he became as immersed in his photography as the surfboard business.

Farther down the coast, in 1989, Debbie Bell and Randy Hall started up Rodanthe Surf Shop, featuring Hatteras Glass Surfboards. They made and sold boards and had a ding repair service. In 1995, it was relocated to its current location, and after many years, the shop was sold to Jason and Lovie Heilig.

WES LAINE JOINS THE WORLD TOUR

In the early 1980s, a member of the local surfing elite turned pro. Wes Laine had started surfing at age six, learning on a ten-foot, two-inch Jacobs his brother Randy had. In 1968, at age eight, he got his first board from Jimbo Brothers, a five-foot, ten-inch V bottom Vardemann. Randy and Wes grew up surfing on 65th street in Virginia Beach, but back in 1970 and 1971, his family lived in Newport, Rhode Island, and he and Randy surfed in the ESA New England district, under Colin "Doc" Couture's leadership.

Nine years older than Wes, Randy made his mark on the tour in the 1970s, winning ESA contests and then working his way in 1976 onto the pro IPS circuit just as it was getting off the ground. In 1977, he climbed in the rankings to twenty-second in the world.

In 1979, Randy Laine was at the Grog's Seaside Pro event in New Jersey, and Wes was there as an amateur. Both ended up competing in the same event in small surf, and Wes won, beating his brother. This was a turning point for Wes, proving he could compete and win. All of a sudden, he was going up against the big boys from the world tour. In the next event, Wes was seeded against world champ Rabbit Bartholomew, who was just off the plane. Wes surfed well, but Rabbit won the contest.

In 1981, Laine won the ECSC pro division over Buddy Pelletier. Then during Christmas break in 1982, Wes flew out to the Katin contest in California. He was a college senior at Virginia Wesleyan with one semester until graduation. Taking fifth place in the contest, he won $2,500 and was offered sponsorship by Rip Curl and a plane ticket to Australia. Wes postponed his last semester in college and went Down Under.

At home, he was sponsored by 17th Street Surf Shop, which was owned by Lee and Harriet Jones, and rode Canyon Surfboards. For two months prior to his trip, he surfed eight hours every day, mostly in junk, just to get ready. Laine's main influence was Mark Richards, and their styles, "with arms flying," were very similar. When Laine got to Australia in March 1982, he had an immediate impact and served notice of his arrival.

At his first contest, he reached only the last round of the trials. However, at the Stubbies contest, he got through the trials and qualified for the main event and drew soon-to-be four-time world champion Mark Richards as his seed. It was man on man, best two out of three. Wes competed well, but MR pulled off a great final wave to win the heat.

The next day, Burleigh Heads was eight-feet classic, with Wes surfing beyond himself. MR did win their second heat, but not without a fight, and Laine went on to beat Australian surf star Cheyne Horan to reach the final. Through this performance, though he did not win, Wes was now considered a contender and earned Rookie of the Contest honors.

At the Bells Beach contest, Wes again surfed well but went down to the number-two seed Rabbit Bartholomew in a split decision. Then it was on for the Coke Surfabout, which offered a lot of prize money. The contest site was moved around according to where the best surf was. Again, Wes drew the number-two seed, Rabbit, and lost a split decision to him.

After Australia, it was off to Africa, Brazil and Hawaii. Wes finished twenty-second in the world in his first year, better than anticipated. He was a sensation in the Gunston and Coke contests and continued to improve during the tour, competing week after week.

In 1983, the young guys—Wes Laine, Willie Morris and Tom Curren—were again making a run at the old guard that included Rabbit, Mark Richards and Ian Cairns. On his home turf, so to speak, Wes won the OP contest in Atlantic City, an ASP event, and got second at Bells Beach, a whisker away from winning. He also got some thirds and fifths on the tour and got a third in Hawaii in the World Cup and seventh in the Pipeline Masters. He was invited to the Duke contest, making it to the quarterfinals. He also surfed in the Eddie Aikiu contest, the only Easterner invited to surf Waimea, held only at twenty-five feet or better, a non-ASP event. He finished ninth that year, his first time in the top ten.

At that time, Tom Curren, who would go on to win three World Championships, was the most talented surfer and a natural surfer. Curren visited the East Coast on several occasions, attending the U.S. Championships in Hatteras in 1974 and 1978, when Laine won the junior men's division. In 1984, Wes finished twelfth, starting out strong but suffering a string of poor results toward the end of the year, dropping from seventh place.

Then in 1985, Laine won the Cape Town Steak Ranch Surfabout in Cape Town, South Africa, an epic event held in the biggest-ever surf for a contest outside Hawaii. On the last day, waves reached twelve to fifteen feet. He captured the surfing world's headlines as an East Coast surfer from Virginia Beach, which only further validated and added to the lore of Virginia Beach surfing, a tradition that started with James Jordan, Babe Braithwaite, John Smith, Bob Holland and Pete Smith.

South Africa offered the benefit of two oceans, the Atlantic and the Indian, and contest organizers could move the contest site to where the best surf was. In this instance, the contest venue was moved from three- to four-foot surf to just around the corner where there was twelve- to fifteen-foot surf.

In the semis, Wes beat Mike Varness of Durban, while Glen Winton beat Mark Occhilupo. It was Laine and Winton in the finals. Wes was hot, on a good board, and while it started out close, he took the lead. Winton was trying to catch up when a wave broke his board, and he never regained his momentum. Wes won the contest.

About this time, Wes began riding a hometown board, Wave Riding Vehicles, shaped by Bill Frierson. For years, Wes had ridden Canyon Surfboards out of San Diego, shaped by Rusty Preisendorfer. Now he still rode Rusty boards but also rode Friersons, with each shaper's boards complementing the other in different surf conditions. By 1987, Wes began to wind down his professional surfing career, and 1988 was his last year on the tour. He was ranked nineteenth in 1987 and twenty-eighth in 1988.

During that early to mid-1980s era, Laine was the most successful East Coast surfer on the world tour, bolstering and bringing to light the prominent surfing history of Virginia Beach that dated back to the very beginning.

Chapter 5

1990-2020

Closing Out

The 1990s rolled in on the cusp of a new era of soul surfing as longboards made a comeback, bringing with them an elegant style of surfing that resurrected walking to the nose and "hanging ten." Longboard shapers and surfers from the 1960s now had an opportunity to bring back old styles and create new ones.

The 1990s and 2000s really cemented the reputation of the Outer Banks of North Carolina as an eastern training and proving ground for future world champion Hall of Fame surfers. In 1991, future 2001 world champ C.J. Hobgood was the Menehune ESA champ. At the twenty-fifth annual contest in 1992, six-time ESA champion Kelly Slater returned to Hatteras as the ASP world champion. Two years later, in 1994, former ESA, NSSA and U.S. champ Lisa Anderson from Ormond Beach won the first of her four straight ASP world titles. This was all after Floridian Frieda Zamba won her four world titles in the 1980s.

Remarkably, Slater racked up five more world title crowns from 1994 to 1998, then five more championships *after that* in 2005, 2006, 2008, 2010 and 2011. In total, Slater has won eleven world titles, the all-time greatest competitive surfer. It all started on the ESA contest circuit that for the most part ended each year in Buxton at the lighthouse for the ESA Championships.

That is, until they moved the lighthouse and eventually the contest. Due to challenges with advertising and merchandising on National Park land, and securing permits for the event, the contest finally moved to Nags Head,

A surfer south of the Nags Head Pier finds good waves after Hurricane Bertha in late July 1990. *Photo by Drew Wilson, courtesy of the Outer Banks History Center.*

where there were fewer restrictions and wider access to accommodations and amenities for the weeklong event.

In 1999, the lighthouse was moved from its historic perch where it had stood since 1870, about a mile parallel to the ocean, toward Cape Point. For a long time, the lighthouse was extremely vulnerable to beach erosion. When it was built and through much of the twentieth century, there were hundreds of yards of beach. By the 1990s, the lighthouse had been exposed to many storms and hurricanes that finally left no alternative—other than letting the lighthouse fall into the sea—but to move it.

The Surfrider Foundation was founded in Malibu in 1984 and mainly focused on water issues in California. In 1990, Scott Roher of Virginia Beach and Rob Beedie, a Portsmouth native and lifelong surfer, organized the showing of *Surfer the Movie* at the Commodore Theater in Portsmouth. This played an important role as a fundraiser in getting the Surfrider Foundation underway on the East Coast. In 1991, Virginia became the first chapter of the East Coast Surfrider Foundation with 132 members, followed soon after by the second chapter opened on the Outer Banks. In 1995, Gray's Department Store earned the prestigious Blue Water Award.

In 1996, the inaugural induction ceremony of the East Coast Surf Legends Hall of Fame was held, with Bob Holland, Pete Smith and Bob White from Virginia Beach honored. Other honorees, almost all with ties to the early East Coast Surfing Championships, were Dick Catri, Claude Codgen, Colin "Doc" Couture, John Hannon, Cecil Lear, Mimi Munro, Jack Murphy, Gary Propper, David Reese, Yancy Spencer, Mike Tabeling and Bruce Valluzzi.

Since then, more than a dozen additional honorees from Virginia Beach and the Outer Banks have been inducted. From Virginia Beach, these include John Smith, Dusty Hinnant, Babe Braithwaite, Fred Grosskruetz, Bill Frierson, Les Shaw, Wes Laine and Jason Borte. From North Carolina, they are Ted James, Scott Busbey and Mickey McCarthy. Some other notables with direct ties but from outside Virginia Beach and the Outer Banks are Greg Loehr, Ricky Rasmussen, Buddy Pelletier and Will Allison.

The first class of the East Coast Surf Legends Hall of Fame was inducted in 1996. Most inductees, if not all, had direct ties to Virginia Beach and the Outer Banks. *Back row, left to right*: Dick Catri, Jack Murphy, Bob Holland, Mimi Munro, Greg Noll, Claude Codgen, Dan Heritage and Pete Smith. *Front row*: Yancey Spencer, David Reese, Pat O'Hare, Peter Pan, Gary Propper, Cecil Lear and John Hannon. *Courtesy of Pete Smith.*

In 1997, Bob Holland was honored yet again, this time by being inducted into the Virginia Sports Hall of Fame.

On the Outer Banks, the older guys started inspiring a new generation of up-and-coming surfers. Lynn Shell, Mickey McCarthy, Billy Diggs, Barry Price and Stuart Taylor all were accomplished surfers who had traveled and proven themselves in big surf. By the 1990s, a new generation of home-grown talent was breaking out on the Outer Banks.

Noah Snyder from Kill Devil Hills started surfing in 1985 when he was twelve and came up through the ESA competitive circuit; 3rd Street was his stomping ground. Only a year or so later, WRV sponsored him, and Lynn Shell started shaping his surfboards.

Snyder went to Hawaii for the first time in 1990 with Shell. Four years later, in 1994, Snyder turned pro at age twenty-one and competed in events including the Florida Pro and ECSC. He became a professional surfer, traveling for photo shoots to exotic surfing locales. Spurred partly by Mickey McCarthy's photos, Snyder started getting his images in the magazines from trips to Indonesia and other places. In 2004, a documentary called *Noah's Arc* was released, profiling the great surfing and the deep Christian faith of Noah Snyder, Jesse Hines, Brad Beacham and many others in the surfing community.

Jesse Hines from Kitty Hawk was a few years younger than Snyder and followed in his footsteps. He, too, grew up competing in the ESA, with Jim Vaughn at Whalebone Surf Shop an early sponsor. In 1993, Hines won the boys' division of the VB/OBX Challenge in Frisco, and Shell helped him secure sponsorship from Hawaiian Island Creations (HIC), where Shell had a line of surfboards. Hines then picked up sponsorship from O'Neill Wetsuits. After winning the Red Bull Nova Scotia contest, Hines started getting travel assignments for surf photo shoots in France, Yemen, Iceland, Japan and Alaska. He made the cover of all the major surf mags, including *Waves*, *TransWorld Surf*, *Surfer* and *Surfing* magazines. For several years while a pro surfer, he lived in California before moving back. He also had a successful modeling career for companies like Abercrombie and Fitch, Polo and J. Crew.

Matt Beacham and Billy Hume went pro in the 2000s, much like their compatriots Snyder and Hines. Along with Snyder, Hines and Matt and Brad Beacham were Matt Pruett, Brent McCoy and Craig Watson. Matt Beacham also became known for his series *New Pollution*, which chronicled young athletes. Another standout was Brett Barley from Buxton, who distinguished himself in Hawaii. None other than Gerry Lopez, the pipeline

Right: Jay Ellis of Nags Head, July 24, 1990. *Photo by Drew Wilson, courtesy of the Outer Banks History Center.*

Below: Brian Sullivan of Kill Devil Hills braves cold winter waters to catch the big swell near the Avalon Pier in 1990. *Photo by Drew Wilson, courtesy of the Outer Banks History Center.*

master, nicknamed him "Knarly Barley." Along with them came the McManus brothers, Pat, Dean and Heath, from South Nags Head.

Farther south, though not from the Outer Banks, was Ben Bourgeois from Wrightsville Beach. As a former ESA champion, he spent a lot of time on the Outer Banks and was the first North Carolina surfer to make the ASP world tour, from which he retired in 2008. He made a name when he won the Quicksilver Grom Invitational in 1995 and then the ISA World Junior title in 1996, which qualified him for the world tour. But after he retired in 2008, he told *Surfer* magazine that he was eager to get home and to get back to the Outer Banks. "Next year, I'm not gonna miss a swell in Hatteras."

In Virginia Beach, Jason Borte started winning local contests, including ECSC. Ultimately, he became an ESA All-Star and then won the ASP East Championship in 1997. Borte also became a chronicler of surfing. When it came for the all-time greatest surfer, Kelly Slater, to write his memoirs, *Pipe Dreams: A Surfer's Journal*, in 2004, it was Jason Borte who was his coauthor.

After graduating from First Colonial High School, Tim Nolte did ding repair in Virginia Beach, where he grew up, and then started his own factory. He built boards there from 1984 until moving to the Outer Banks in 2001. He opened a shop in Currituck just over the bridge and builds both surfboards and SUPs. Meanwhile, in 2002, Lynn Shell took over Bert's Surf Shop and changed the name to Outer Banks Boarding Company (OBBC). Also that year, Mike Rowe started Hooked Surfboards featuring his own shapes.

In 2004, the surfboard manufacturing industry fell into a freefall when Grubby Clark, the major foam provider to the industry since the 1950s, decided to quit and close up his business, leaving foam production to collapse. Clark pretty much had a monopoly. All of a sudden, there was nowhere to get blanks.

After the dust settled, a new surfboard industry emerged heavy with Chinese factory-built surfboards using new materials. The suspicion was that the biggest surfboard builder in the world was now a guy in a suit on Wall Street. Epoxy boards increasingly became available with lower price points than hand-shaped fiberglass surfboards. Nevertheless, through the challenges emerged a traditional—if slimmed-down—surfboard operation, with shapers and laminators and sanders and polishers.

WRV increased its presence in the surfing world as it opened stores in Hawaii in 2004 and Puerto Rico in 2008. Surf and Adventure Co., on the way to Sandbridge, which traced its roots to 1974, started producing its own surfboards in 2006 and, for a time, had a retail store at ODU in Norfolk.

Wave Riding Vehicles moved its factory from Virginia Beach to Harbinger, North Carolina, in 1987. *Author's collection.*

Pungo Board House was opened by Dylan and Kari Rogers in 2007 in an old house complete with skateboard halfpipe out back.

The Pit Surf Shop in Kill Devil Hills was founded in 1994 by Ben Sproul and Steve Pauls. They ran it for many years until Missi Dermatas took over the business. In 2016, Todd Kleban opened Banks Surf Supply in Nags Head. In 2019, Sproul became mayor of Kill Devil Hills. Surfers were now political and business leaders and pillars of the community.

Meanwhile, the East Coast Surfing Championships in Virginia Beach continued to grow. The contest typically offered $100,000 in prize money, one of the best purses on the circuit, and it was a must stop to maintain points on the qualifying pro tour leading to the World Surf League (WSL) world tour. Professional surfers from Peru, Brazil, Australia and, of course, California and Hawaii came to Virginia Beach each August for the contest.

In 1997, future 2001 WSL world champ C.J. Hobgood won the Pro Junior division at ECSC in Virginia Beach. Californian Joel Tudor won the Pro Longboard division, followed by Steven Slater (brother of Kelly).

Tom Curren, one of the all-time great pro surfers, a three-time world champ, won the ECSC pro division in 1998. Linda Davoli from Brigantine, New Jersey, at one time the number-three women's surfer in the world back

Pat and Heath McManus of South Nags Head prepare to compete in the ESA Surfing Championships at the Cape Hatteras Lighthouse in September 1990. *Photo by Drew Wilson, courtesy of the Outer Banks History Center.*

An unidentified surfer powers through a turn, creating the spray behind him. *Photo by Drew Wilson, courtesy of the Outer Banks History Center.*

in 1980, won the ECSC senior women's event in 1999. Bobby Holland won senior longboard the same year. In 2000, George Desgain won the legends' division.

California surf bad boy Dino Andino won the pro men's in 2002 and Falina Spires the pro women's. That same year, Chip McQuilkin won the legends' division. And on the women's pro world circuit, future surf star Courtney Conlogue from California won in 2006 in Virginia Beach before going to two runner-up finishes in the world title chase in 2015 and 2016. The same year, Virginia Beach ECSC champion surfer Seth Broudy won the senior men's. In 2011, ASP junior pro Nat Young from Santa Cruz came in first.

Paul West became the ESA Virginia Beach district director and was also competition director of ECSC for thirty years. In 1998, he was appointed competition director for the USSF. While ECSC and the ESA contest format continued to be benchmarks of competitive surfing, some new marquee contests were established.

In 2004, the Steel Pier Classic Surfing Contest, run by the Virginia Longboard Federation, was founded and held over the Memorial Day weekend. It was a longboard contest primarily and named in honor of the old Steel Pier, site of almost a decade of East Coast Surfing Championships before being destroyed by hurricane surf and torn down in 1977. The contest evolved over the years to include shortboards and SUPs and also expanded into a local high school art and surf art show.

In October 2008, the WRV Battle of the Banks was held in Rodanthe with an overhead swell with offshore winds. The contest pitted Virginia Beach against the Outer Banks, a rivalry one could say, with two teams of six for each side. The final six-man contest pitted Noah Snyder, Jesse Hines and Pat McManus from the Outer Banks against Andrew Meyer, Jason Borte and Lucas Rogers. Virginia Beach won the team event, and McManus took the individual honors. Best barrel went to Hines.

Founded in 2009, the WRV Pro earned its place as an official WSL men's and women's qualifier event, which meant it drew top talent worldwide. In order to surf the best waves possible, it sets up a window in which to run the contest.

In Virginia Beach, Coastal Edge opened its first store in 1990, owned by Deepak Nachnani. In 2009, Coastal Edge took over the title sponsorship of the East Coast Surfing Championships. On the Outer Banks, Gary Smith opened Corolla Surf Shop in 1996. The shop also functions as a museum with a large display of classic and historic surfboards from the collection

Right: The Steel Pier Classic surf contest in Virginia Beach, founded in 2004 under the auspices of the Virginia Longboard Federation, began a new tradition of longboard surfing competition. *Author's collection.*

Below: The 1991 ESA men's champion, Seth Broudy of Virginia Beach, wipes out on a wave in Nags Head after a powerful cutback. *Photo by Drew Wilson, courtesy of the Outer Banks History Center.*

of Steve Wise. Other shops established locations there, including Island Revolution Surf Company and Kitty Hawk Surf Company. In Duck, Outer Banks Surf Shop and Duck Village Outfitters offered surfboards and lessons.

The fight for beach access continued in Duck in 2019 when Bob Hovey, owner of Duck Village Outfitters, was charged with criminal trespassing at the Seabreeze beach access. He was confronted by property owners demanding his arrest, saying that the Sand Dollar Shores Homeowners Association controlled that beach access, that it was private and that he was not allowed to use it. In February 2020, a judge for the North Carolina Superior Court ruled in favor of Hovey that beach access was public.

In 2017, the Eastern Surfing Association celebrated its fiftieth anniversary. During that half century, the ESA had attracted upward of 100,000 members through the organization, was now organized into twenty-four districts with 49 volunteer board members and had awarded over $150,000 via the Bette Marsh Scholarship Fund. With over 7,000 surfers, the ESA is recognized as the world's largest amateur surfing organization.

The ESA and the World Surf League in 2019 reached an agreement to allow eight East Coast surfers a path to earn slots in the World Qualifying Series (WQS), the gateway to the WSL world pro tour.

A cloudy day during a contest. *Photo by Drew Wilson, courtesy of the Outer Banks History Center.*

Ed Fawess, of the New York district, competes at the ESA Surfing Championships in September 1990. *Photo by Drew Wilson, courtesy of the Outer Banks History Center.*

To assess the worthiness of such an agreement, one only need look at the twenty World Championships earned by East Coast surfers, including both the men's and women's circuits: eleven by Kelly Slater, four by Frieda Zamba, four by Kathy Anderson and one by C.J. Hobgood—all Floridians, and all of whom at one time or another competed in Virginia Beach and the Outer Banks. These numbers of course don't include the many other East Coast surfers who have competed on the top international professional tour.

As noted in *Surfer* magazine, the WSL "struck a partnership to help clear a path for more East Coast surfers and signaled a new era for the renowned East Coast amateur surfing circuit….For decades the Eastern Surfing Association was, organizationally speaking, the U.S. premier amateur surfing circuit, far ahead of California's amateur contest organizations, grooming generations of East Coast surfers despite the region's 'inferior' waves and to help establish the Right Coast as a formidable feeder territory for international surf stars."

One of the most recent up-and-coming stars was Rachel Wilson from Virginia Beach, ranked thirty-third in the world in 2019. Yet the East had

Above: Lynn Shell opened the Outer Banks Boarding Company in 2003. *Author's collection.*

Left: The 2019 ESA Outer Banks district contest schedule is posted. *Author's collection.*

Fifty years after the original photo was taken in 1962 of Virginia Beach surfers who traveled to Gilgo Beach, the same surfers gathered together for a reenactment. *Left to right*: Joe Potter, Mr. Potter, Wayne Morgan, Jimmy Gregory, Nicky Michaels, Butch Maloney, Norman Morse, Jimpe Holland, Tommy Lueke, Ron Smith, Richard Neal and Pete Smith (*standing*). *Courtesy of Pete Smith.*

Above: Bob Crutchfield at Pea Island on March 12, 1989. *Photo by Drew Wilson, courtesy of the Outer Banks History Center.*

Left: Mickey McCarthy of New Sun Surfboards. *Photo by Drew Wilson, courtesy of the Outer Banks History Center.*

distinguished itself in more ways than just competition. In 2019, Bill Frierson was awarded a place in the International Surfboard Builders Hall of Fame in Huntington Beach, nominated by Scott Busbey, himself a member.

By 2020, the East Coast Surfing Championships was a weeklong contest and festival that drew hundreds of pro and amateur surf competitors from around the nation and around the world. As reported in *USA Today*, "The ECSC has been drawing top surf talent to Virginia Beach for the past five decades. 'What makes Virginia Beach special is that it's the epicenter of the surf industry here,' said Chase Pittman. 'The ECSC is the largest part about that. Anytime you get the world's best surfers traveling to a place, it elevates the talent level. We have this wonderful mix of influences here that has created a bunch of world class surfers. Through the course of the week an estimated 100,000 people take in the event, which also includes music, skateboarding, and other events.'"

One can only conclude that Virginia Beach and the Outer Banks, both separately and together, and each in significant ways, have earned their reputation as an epic center of East Coast surfing.

Selected Bibliography

Books

Bickford, Christopher. *Legends of the Sandbar: A Life of Surf on the Outer Banks*. BurnBooks/David Alan Harvey, 2017.

Callis, Ann Hanbury, and Danna Cullen. *Vintage North End Virginia Beach: An Illustrated History*. Atglen, PA: Schiffer Publishing, 2012.

Finney, Ben, and James D. Houston. *Surfing: A History of the Ancient Hawaiian Sport*. Rohnert Park, CA: Pomegranate Artbooks, 1996.

Hairr, John, and Ben Wunderly. *Surfing NC: A Timeline of the History of the Sport of Surfing in North Carolina*. N.p.: North Carolina Maritime Museum, 2015.

Jennings, Chris, and Hank Gardner. *From the Beach to the Bay: An Illustrated History of Sandbridge in Virginia*. Virginia Beach, VA: Donning Company/Publishers, 2000.

Jordan, James M., and Frederick S. Jordan. *Virginia Beach: A Pictorial History*. Richmond, VA: Hale Publishing, 1974.

Lynch, Gary, and Malcolm Gault-Williams. *Tom Blake: The Uncommon Journey of a Pioneer Waterman*. 2nd ed. N.p.: Croul Publications, 2013.

Mansfield, Stephen S. *Princess Anne County and Virginia Beach: A Pictorial History*. Virginia Beach, VA: Donning Company Publishers, 1989.

Slater, Kelly, with Jason Borte. *Pipe Dreams: A Surfer's Journey*. New York: Regan Books, 2003.

Warshaw, Matt. *Surfrider in Search of the Perfect Wave*. New York: Harper, 1997.

Young, Nat, with Graig McGregor. *The History of Surfing*. Tucson, AZ: Body Press, 1983.

Magazines

Atlantic Surfing. Paul Chapey and John Gunderson, Brooklyn, NY, 1965.

Competition Surf. Ed Greevy and James F. Joiner. Plainview, NY, 1966–67.

Eastern Surf Magazine. Tom Dugan and Dick Meseroll. Melbourne Beach, FL, 1991–2020.

International Surfing. John Peterson. CA, 1965.

Surf. Mike Mann and Allan Margolis. Indialantic, FL, 1977–79.

Surfer. John Severson. San Clemente, CA, 1960–2020.

Surfing East. Richard S. Van Winkle. Ridgewood, NJ, 1965–67.

Wave Rider. John Griffin. Cocoa Beach, FL, 1975–82.

Index

About the Author

Tony Lillis started skateboarding and surfing as a teenager in the mid-1970s. One of his most formative experiences was a two-week surfing and camping trip to Cape Hatteras in 1978. He enjoyed it so much he transferred from a college near the mountains in Pennsylvania to Old Dominion University in Norfolk, where he earned a bachelor's in history and made frequent jaunts to the Virginia Beach oceanfront before and after class, and to the Outer Banks as often as possible. After graduation, he worked in book publishing for thirty years as an editor, marketing director and project manager. For many years, he was a resident of Virginia Beach and now resides in Norfolk.